SAY IT IN MAORI

MAORI PHRASE BOOK
Compiled by Alan Armstrong

Published by Viking Sevenseas Limited
P.O. Box 152 Paraparaumu, New Zealand.

Alan Armstrong was an Auckland businessman. He was a former Chairman and Club Captain of the famous Ngati Poneke Young Maori Club of Wellington and had trained and led several Maori concert parties which have appeared overseas. His wife, Te Waiehu, had often collaborated with him in his concert party work and is a grand daughter of the late Sir Apirana Ngata. Alan Armstrong was the author of a number of publications:

"*Maori Action Songs*" (with Reupena Ngata)
"*Maori Games and Haka*"
"*The Maori People*"
"*Say it in Maori*"
"*Maori Customs and Crafts*"
"*Kiwi Cooking*"
"*Haere Mai*"
"*Games and Dances of the Maori People*"
"*Nga Mahi Takaro a te Maori*"

THIRTEENTH PRINTING 2005
ISBN 0854670106

Graphic

© Copyright 1968 Seven Seas Publishing Pty Ltd,
PO Box 152, Paraparaumu, New Zealand
PRINTED IN HONG KONG
BY G.L. Graphic & Printing LTD.

CONTENTS

SECTION 1
The Maori language 5
*Introduction; Nature of the language;
Tribal differences; Transliteration*

SECTION 2
Maori pronunciation 9
Vowels; Consonants; Syllables; Emphasis

SECTION 3
Vocabulary 11
Using the vocabulary; Maori–English; English–Maori

SECTION 4
Conversational phrases 36
*Greetings, thanks, courtesy phrases;
Eating and drinking; Of work and doing things; Coming and going;
Seeking directions; Expressing emotions; Weather;
Enquiries; Negatives, affirmatives and short replies;
Speaking, hearing and listening; Telling the time;
Counting; Days, months, seasons, compass points*

SECTION 5
Proverbial sayings 48

SECTION 6
Place names and their meanings 51

SECTION 7
Miscellaneous 55
*Common English names and their Maori equivalents;
New Zealand currency and metric conversion;
Kiwi English and pronunciation*

Colour Plates

Wanganui Pa in the 1840's (Gilfillian) **15**
Pohutukawa flowers in bloom **21**
Maori mother and child **31**
Toi toi plants near Lake Waikaremoana **40**
Statue of Pania, Napier **46**

Etchings by C. D. Barraud reproduced on
pages 4, 8, 10, 12, 26, 35, 44, 47 and 54
appeared originally in 'New Zealand,
Graphic and Descriptive' published in 1877

Te Voor

THE MAORI LANGUAGE

Introduction
The visitor to New Zealand will not need a phrase book to converse with Maori or Pakeha (white person) provided he or she speaks English! English is the nation's official language and is the medium of instruction in all its schools. Some of the finest exponents of English in New Zealand are Maoris and all except a mere handful of the very oldest Maoris speak, read and write English in the same manner as their European or Pakeha brethren.

Nevertheless Maori is still very much a living language and is widely used in Maori homes and on purely Maori social occasions. It is a subject at University level and is sat in public examinations by a large number of pupils each year. It is true the increasing urbanisation of the Maori people is bringing forth a new generation with very little opportunity to appreciate at first hand the values and cultural traditions of their forbears yet there are few Maoris who would not assert that even now their language is the corner stone of their identity as a proud warrior race.

Maori is not an easy language to learn. It has a rich vocabulary and a complex but by no means illogical grammatical structure. It would be impossible for a visitor either to learn the language before coming to New Zealand or to pick it up during the course of a stay of any length except the longest duration and then only if his contact with the Maori people was of the most intimate kind. Maoris would never expect a visitor to address them in their own language and it is perhaps for that very reason that a visitor who cared to try would be richly rewarded with trust, understanding and warm friendship.

This booklet offers the means to understand something of the nature of the language, to be able to pronounce it in a reasonably accurate fashion, to know a very inadequate vocabulary and to learn a few phrases which properly and appropriately used could be an entree into Maori social life and a friendship with the Maori people which would be both richly rewarding and warmly satisfying.

The nature of the language
The Maori language is phonetic, that is, it is pronounced generally speaking, as it is spelt. There are fifteen letters in the Maori alphabet. The vowels are a, e, i, o, u and the consonants are h, k, m, n, ng, p, r, t, w, wh. The sounds "ng" and "wh" have been classed as letters because they form single sounds which are not represented exactly in the English language.

Maori is a dialect of the language spoken throughout Polynesia. As such it has an affinity with most of the languages spoken in the Pacific and in South-East Asia. For example:

	Maori	Fiji	Samoa	Solomon Is	Malaya	Tahiti
Sky	rangi	lagi	lagi	dangi	langit	ra'i
Stone	whatu	vatu	fatu	vatu	batu	fatu
Eye	mata	mata	mata	mata	mata	mata
Five	rima	lima	lima	lima	lima	rima

Within the language itself there are differences between tribes and districts but these are lessening with the passage of time and do not prevent Maoris throughout New Zealand from understanding one another.

Tribal differences in spoken Maori
Between the various tribes there are differences in emphasis and intonation. In some areas Maoris speak in a sing-song manner and in others they speak more quickly biting the words out in staccato fashion. The "wh" sound is often a sure pointer to a speaker's tribe. It is variously rendered as "wh", "h", "hw" and "f". Amongst the Tuhoe people of the Bay of Plenty and in parts of the South Island the "ng" sound becomes a straight "n". The Ngai Tahu people substitute "k" for "ng" in many words. Thus "kainga" becomes "kaika".

There are also minor differences in vocabulary and some tribes are more addicted than others to transliterate forms and to the interjection in Maori speech of English words and phrases. This latter is an increasingly modern tendency deplored by the dwindling band of traditionalists and recognised by others as a mark of true bilingualism where speakers are equally at home in two languages and use that which better expresses the particular thought at a particular point in the flow of conversation.

As an example of minor tribal vocabulary variation we have the Maori equivalent of the English "friend", "sir", or "old chap". The most common Maori term of address is "e hoa" (literally: "oh friend"). However "e kare" is the equivalent amongst the people of the Waikato. On the East Coast of the North Island however one would hear "e hika". Two other terms of address used in certain areas are "e mara" for both sexes and "e kare" for older men only. A common Maori greeting is "Kei te pewhea koe" (How are you doing). However, many a Maori visiting the Ngati Porou tribal area might be somewhat mystified to be greeted with "Kei t'aha?". The speaker still means "How are you doing" but in reality he is using an abbreviated form of "Kei te aha koe" which is "*What* are you doing?" or How are you?

Transliteration
Before the coming of the Europeans, the vocabulary of the Maori language was naturally smaller than it is today. Colonisation brought many things which were new to the Maoris and they listened carefully to the European names of these things and then tried to repeat the words. This conversion of English words into Maori is called transliteration. The transliterate forms varied. Many of the terms stuck and are listed in the dictionary as the Maori words for importations unknown to the ancient Maori. For example, "huka" is sugar, "poaka" is pig, "pene" is pen and there are many others. Most of the Maori words are easy to relate to their English equivalent but a few are a little strange and interesting. "Wiwi" is Frenchman and derives from the French "oui, oui". "Taika" is the word for a piebald horse and this is due to the fact that Governor Grey had a piebald pony named "Tiger".

Some purists deplore the use of transliterate words but this is a quite legitimate facet of linguistic evolution. Just as many English words have been borrowed from foreign sources so the Maori has coined words from the other language with which he lives. (One interesting example of transliteration in reverse is that the pioneers on hearing the quick Maori pronunciation of "pohutukawa" christened the tree of this name "footy-cover".)

Of course many words in modern Maori are only found in a transliterate form of the English. Where a Maori word exists however it should be used in preference to a transliterate form. In some cases however the traditional word carries a different nuance of meaning from its modern equivalent. For example the transliterate form of cook is "kuki". The old Maori word however is "tuamu". This also means a slave because cooking, as a menial task, was normally given to slaves to carry out. There is another word which can be used if "tumau" is considered to be indicative of a buried past. This is "kaiwhakamaoa kai" which literally means "the worker who cooks food." Most dictionaries give the word for window as "mataaho" or "matapihi", but the transliterations "winera" and "wini" are quite acceptable as these apply to a glass window whereas the older words really mean the opening in the wall of an old-time meeting house closed by a sort of sliding panel.

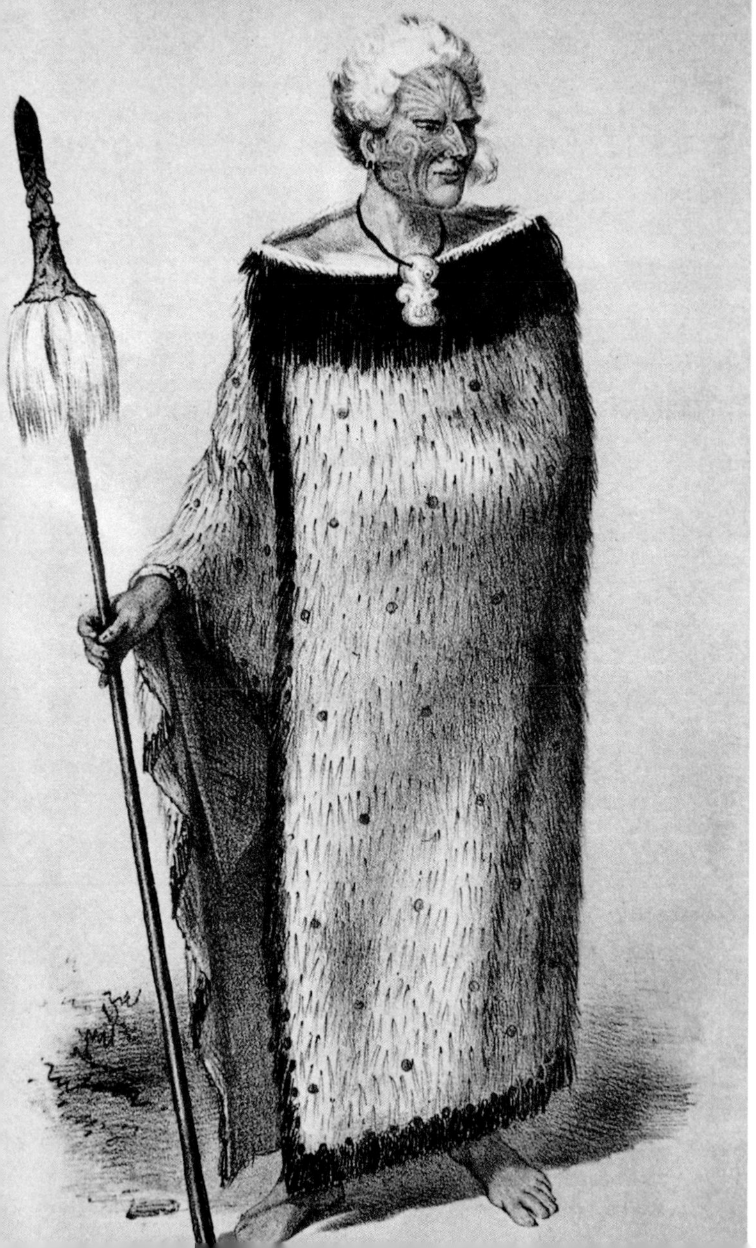

THE PRONUNCIATION OF MAORI

We give greatly simplified rules for the pronunciation of Maori. Whilst it is a fact that only a person who has studied Maori for a very long time can pronounce it as perfectly as a native speaker of the language, this applies to any language. It is possible however with only a little care to pronounce the language correctly and in a way which is pleasing to the Maori ear.

Each vowel has a short and a long sound and the use of one or the other of these sounds can completely alter the meaning of the word. For example kākā (or kaakaa) is the Maori parrot whilst kāka is another native bird, the bittern. Kakā is red hot and kaka means lineage. There has been some controversy as to whether in the written form of the language the lengthened vowel should be shown by the macron, as above, or by a doubling of the letter but most experts agree that there should be some way. The writer prefers the macron as there are occasions in compound words when the doubled vowel is integral to the word rather than a device to indicate length of sound. For example we have "whakaae" which is the causative prefix "whaka" used before the word "ae". Others complain that the doubled vowel distorts the commonly accepted appearance of the word.

Vowels
The approximate sounds are:
- a — as in mark (long "a") or as in cut (short "a")
- e — as in bet (short "e") or a sound in between bet and weight (long "e")
- i — as in feed (long "i") or as in fit (short "i")
- o — as in fork (long "o") or as in violet (short "o")
- u — as in spoon (long "u") or as in soot (short "u")

Maori vowel sounds are very much more pure and rounded than the English equivalents.

Consonants
These are pronounced much the same as in English. The following points should be noted.
- r — The "r" is not rolled.
- ng — This is a nasalised sound as in si*ng*ing. It must NOT be pronounced as a straight "n" sound or as the "ng" in finger.

wh — Whilst in some parts of New Zealand, particularly in the Fa North, "wh" is still given the pronuciation which was undoubtedly current when the missionaries first transcribed Maori into written form namely as an aspirated w (hw as in *when*), the pronunciation of "wh" as a glided-over "f" is now definitely the more common.

Syllables
A beginner attempting to pronounce Maori should divide difficult words into syllables and pronounce each syllable slowly at first and then more quickly until the whole word flows smoothly. A syllable in Maori is *either* a vowel on its own *or* a consonant followed by a vowel ("wh" and "ng" count as single consonants).

Examples are:
 Ngaruawahia — Nga / ru / a / wa / hi / a
 Whangarei — Wha / nga / re / i (NOT Wong - gar - ray)

Emphasis
Maori words are generally emphasised slightly on the first syllable, e.g. *ta*ngata. Some compound words are given a greater degree on the second portion of the word, e.g. *wha*ka*ho*ki.

USING THE VOCABULARY

The latest edition of Williams Maori–English Dictionary (there is no full-scale English–Maori dictionary) runs into almost 500 pages. It will therefore be appreciated just how few words from the total Maori vocabulary can be given in the pages that follow. A selection has been made of common words and of the common meaning or meanings of these words. The vocabulary should thus prove of assistance in reading notices, inscriptions etc. written in Maori and permit limited substitution of key words in the colloquial sentences to be found elsewhere in this book. The abbreviations, and a few words of explanation for those of you who are shaky in English grammar, are as follows:

n = noun i.e. a naming word such as cat, dog etc. As in English Maori nouns are usually preceded by an article "he" (a) "te" (the — singular) "nga" (the — plural) or a demonstrative "tenei" (this) "enei" (these) " tena" (that–which is near the person spoken to) "ena" (plural of tena) "tera" (that — away from you *and* the person spoken to) "era" (plural of tera). In Maori, except for a very few words, the word does NOT change to indicate plural. Thus: *te* tangata (the *man*), *nga* tangata (the *men*).

v.t. = transitive verb. That is, a "doing" word in which the action passes to an object.

v.i. = intransitive verb. A "doing" word in which the action does not pass to an object. Maori is less complex than English and there is not the wide range of tenses to be found in the latter. Tense is usually indicated by other words in the sentence such as "now" "tomorrow" "later" etc. Here are some examples in brief as listed in Williams using the verb "karanga" (to call).

Continuous (past, present, future)   E . . . . ana
         e.g. E karanga ana ia (He was, is, will be, calling)
Completed (past, present, future)   Kua . . . .
         e.g. Kua karanga ia (He had, has, will have, called)
Inceptive (past or future)   Ka . . . .
         e.g. Ka karanga ia (He called, he will call)
Indefinite (past)   I . . . .
         e.g. I karanga ia (He called)
Indefinite (future)   E . . . .
         e.g. E karanga ia (he will call)
Imperative   Karanga! Call!
         Kaua e karanga! Don't call!

- adj. = adjectives i.e. "describing" words. In Maori the adjective always follows its noun, e.g. he whare *nui* (a large house). Two adjectives are not put together with a noun in Maori. Instead the noun is repeated, e.g. He tangata roa, he tangata Pakeha (a tall white man). To compare we add atu (comparative) and rawa (superlative), e.g. pai; pai atu; pai rawa (good; better; best).
- adv. = adverbs i.e. words which describe verbs, adjectives and other adverbs. In the great majority of cases they are placed after the word they qualify. The exceptions are tino (very) ata (slowly) matua (first).

    e.g. He kotiro ataahua *rawa* (the adverb "rawa" qualifies "ataahua") *but* He tamaiti *tino* ataahua ("tino" precedes "ataahua").

- prep. = preposition.
- l.n. = local noun.
- pron. = pronoun i.e. a word which stands for a noun such as "it", "he" etc.
- conj. = conjunction e.g. a "joining" word used to connect two phrases or clauses.
- interr. = interrogative.
- pl. = plural.
- sing. = singular.

MAORI TO ENGLISH

a 1. of, belonging to; 2. a nominal particle
ā (*v.t.*) drive
ā (*conj.*) and; at length
ae (*adv.*) yes
aha (*pron.*) what
ahakoa (*conj.*) although; notwithstanding
ahau (*pron.*) I; me
āhea (*adv.*) when (future)
āhei (*v.i.*) can; be able (not followed by prep.)
ahi (*n*) fire
ahiahi (*n*) evening
āhua (*n*) form, shape, appearance
āhuareka (*adj.*) pleasant
ahu (*v.i.*) move in a certain direction
āianei (*adv.*) now; today
aituā (*n*) misfortune; accident
aki (*v.t.*) dash
ako (*v.t.*) +**i** learn
    +**ki** teach
āku (*pron.*) pl. of **tāku** — my
ākuanei (*adv.*) now, presently
amo (*v.t.*) carry on shoulder
āna (*pron.*) pl. of **tāna** — his/her
anake (*adv.*) only
anō (*adv.*) again
ao (*v.i.*) dawn
    (*n*) day
āpiti (*v*) put side by side
āpōpō (*adv.*) tomorrow
āporo (*n*) apple
arā (*adv.*) namely, that is to say
ara (*n*) path; way
ārahi (*v.t.*) guide; lead
arero (*n*) tongue
aroha (*v.t.*) (*n*) love
aro (*v.t.*) turn towards
    (*n*) front

aroaro (*n*) front; presence
aronga (*n*) direction
aru (*v.t.*) pursue; follow
ata (*n*) morning; shadow
āta (*adv.*) gently; slowly; quietly
ātaahua (*adj.*) beautiful
atawhai (*adj.*) kind
    (*v.t.*) pity
atua (*n*) god
atu (*adv.*) away (from speaker)
āu (*pron.*) pl. of **tāu** — your
au (*pron.*) I; me (short for **ahau**)
aua (*def.*) pl. of **taua** — those
auahi (*n*) smoke
awa (*n*) channel; river
awaawa (*n*) valley
awatea (*n*) daylight
awhi (*v.t.*) embrace
āwhio (*v.t.*) go round
āwhiowhio (*adj.*) winding; circuitous

E

ehara (*adv.*) not
e (*prep.*) verbal particle and particle of address. e.g. e hoa! Friend!
e (*prep.*) by (after passive verbs)
ēhea (*pron*) pl. of **tēhea** — which
eke (*v.t.*) embark; mount
ēna pl. of **tēnā** — those (things close to you)
ēnei pl. of **tēnei** — these
ēngari (*conj.*) but
ērā pl. of **tērā** — those (things over there)
ētahi pl. of **tētahi** — some

H

hahae (*v.t.*) be jealous; have ill-feeling
haehae (*v.t.*) tear
haere (*v.i.*) go; come; walk
haerenga (*n*) journey

13

haereere (*v.i.*) walk about
hāhi (*n*) church
hākari (*n*) feast; large meal
hāmama (*v.i.*) to be open (of the mouth) up (shout)
hanga (*v.t.*) make; build
hāora (*n*) hour
hāpai (*v.t.*) lift
hararei (*n*) holiday
hāte (*n*) shirt
hau (*n*) air; wind
haunga (*n*) smell
haurangi (*adj.*) drunken; distraught
hāwhe (*n; adj.*) half
hē (*n; adj.*) wrong
he a; some
hei (*conj.*) as, for, to be
heke (*v.i.*) migrate; descend
hemokai (*n*) hunger
heoi; heoti (*adv.*) accordingly; that is all; and so
here (*v.t.*) tie
    (*n*) bond
heu (*v.t.*) shave
    (*n*) razor
hia (*interr.*) how many?
hiahia (*v.t.*) wish for; desire
hiainu (*adj.*) thirsty
hiakai (*adj.*) hungry
hiamoe (*adj.*) sleepy
hinengaro (*n*) mind
hinga (*v.i.*) fall
hoa (*n*) friend
hoariri (*n*) enemy
hoatu (*v.t.*) give away; put; place
hōhā (*adj.*) weary; tired of
    (*n*) nuisance
hōhonu (*adj.*) deep
hohoro (*v.i.*) hasten
hōiho horse
hoihoi (*n*) noise
hoki (*conj.*) and, also
    (*v.i.*) return
hoko (*v.t.*) buy, sell
hōmai (*v.t.*) give (to or towards speaker)

hono (*v.t.*) join
hopu (*v.t.*) catch; seize
horoi (*v.t.*) wash
hou (*adj.*) new; fresh
hua (*v.i.*) bear fruit
    (*n*) fruit; berry
hua (*v.t.*) name
huanga (*n*) profit
huarahi (*n*) road
huhua (*adj.*) abundant
huihui (*v*) assemble
huka (*n*) sugar; frost; cold; foam
hukarere (*n*) snow
huri (*v.i.*) turn

I

i (*prep.*) in (also verbal part.)
ia (*pron.*) he; him; she; her
iāri (*n*) yard
iho (*adv.*) downward
ika (*n*) fish
ikeike (*adj.*) high
inā (*conj.*) for; since
    (*adv.*) when
ināhea (*adv.*) when (past)
ināianei (*adv.*) now; just now
inanahi (*adv.*) yesterday
inapō last night
inihi (*n*) inch
inoi (*v.t.*) pray; beg
inu (*v.t.*) drink
ingoa (*n*) name
ipu (*n*) bottle
iti (*adj.*) small
iwi (*n*) nation; people; tribe

K

ka verbal particle
kaha (*adj.*) strong; active
kahaki (*v.t.*) carry off
kāhore (*adv.*) no; not
kahu/kākahu (*n*) garment
kai (*v.t.*) eat
    (*n*) food
kaiārahi (*n*) guide
kaīkā (*adj.*) eager
kaimahi (*n*) one who works
kāinga (*n*) home; unfortified village
kakara (*adj.*) savoury

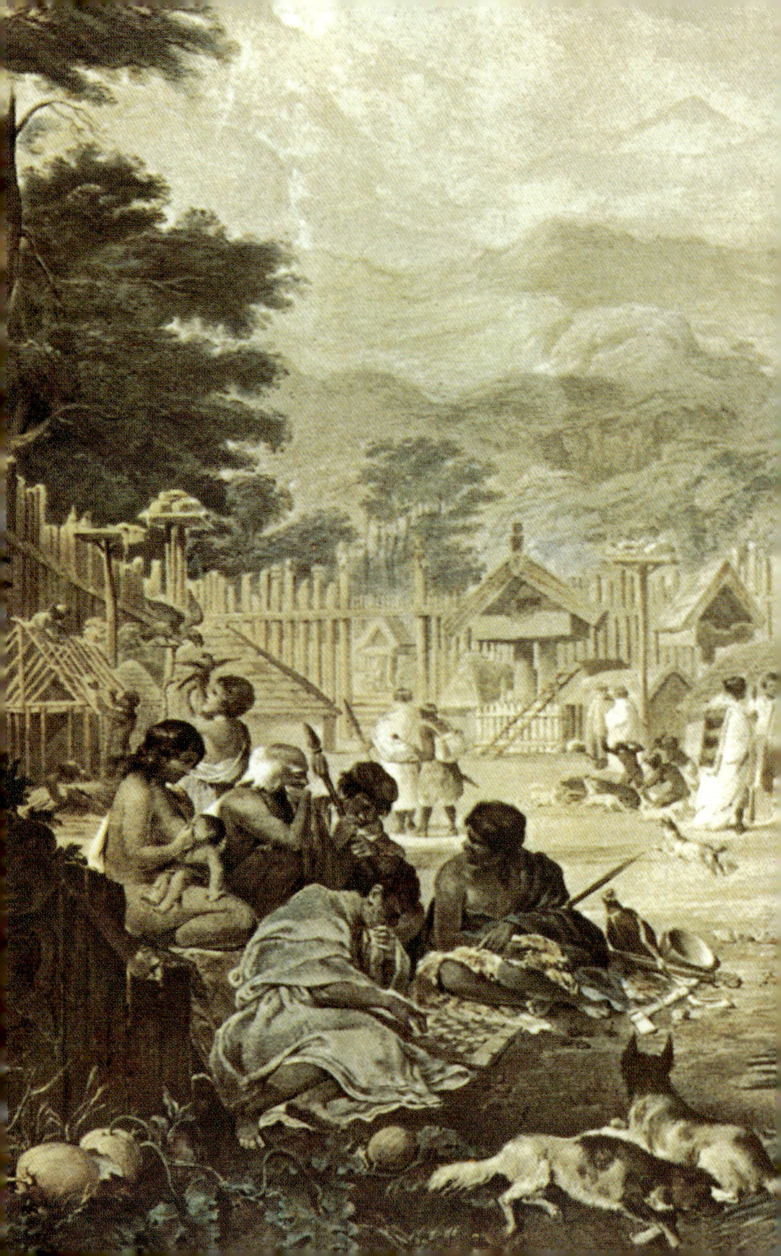

kakawa (*n*) sweat
kake (*v.t.*) ascend
kanikani (*v.i.*) dance
       (*n*) dance
kanohi (*n*) face; eye
kapua (*n*) cloud
karāhe (*n*) glass
karakia (*n*) church service; chant
kararehe (*n*) beast, animal
karanga (*v.t.*) call (out)
karere (*n*) messenger
karu (*n*) eye
kata (*v.i.*) laugh
kāti stop; enough! cease
kātahi (*adv.*) then
kātipa (*n*) constable
katoa (*adj.*) all
     (*n*) whole
kau (*v.t.*) swim
  (*adv.*) only
kaua do not
kauhoe (*v.i.*) swim
kaukau (*v.i.*) bathe
kaumātua (*n*) adult; elder
kaute (*n*) account; bill
   (*v*) to count
kawa (*adj.*) sour; bitter
kawe (*v.t.*) carry; bring; take
kei (*conj.*) lest; that not
  (*prep.*) at; in
keke (*n*) cake
ki (*prep.*) to; at
kī (*v.t.*) say; tell; think
  (*adj.*) full
  (*n*) key
kia (*conj.*) that; in order that
kīano not yet
kīhai (*adv.*) not
kikī (*adj.*) tight
kiko (*n*) flesh; skin
kimi (*v.t.*) seek; look for
kino (*adj.*) bad, ugly
kiri (*n*) skin; bark
kite (*v.t.*) see; understand
kō (*n*) yonder place
ko (*prep.*) to

koa (*adj.*) glad
koe (*pron.*) you (singular)
koi (*adj.*) sharp
konā (*n*) that place (by you)
konei (*n*) this place here
kopa (*n*) corner
kopikopiko (*v.i.*) to go to and fro
korā (*n*) that place over there
kōraha (*n*) open country
kore (*adv.*) not
kōrero (*v.t.*) say; tell
kōrero pukapuka (*v.t.*) read
koroua (*n*) old man
kōrua you two
kotahi (*adj.*) one
kōtiro (*n*) girl
kōwhatu/kōhatu (*n*) stone
kua has, had (verbal part.)
kuiti (*adj.*) narrow
kukume (*v.t.*) pull
kupu (*n*) word; message
kura (*adj.*) red; precious
   (*n*) school
kurī (*n*) dog
kūware (*adj.*) ignorant
kūwaha (*n*) door

M

mā (*adj.*) white; clean; clear
mā (*prep.*) for
māeneene (*adj.*) smooth; soft
māero (*n*) mile
māha (*adj.*) many, contented
mahana (*adj.*) warm
mahara (*v.t.*) think of; remember
mahi (*v.t.*) (*v.i.*) work
mahue (*part.*) left behind
māhunga (*n*) head
mai (*adv.*) hither; towards me
maka (*v.t.*) put; throw; place
mokemoke (*adj.*) lonely
mākona (*part.*) satisfied
māku (*pron.*) for me
mākūkū (*adj.*) damp; wet
māmā (*adj.*) light weighted
  (*n.*) mother
mamae (*n*) pain; anguish

16

mana (*n*) authority; prestige
māna (*pron.*) for him/her
manawa (*n*) heart; mind; breath
manene (*n*) stranger
mano (*n*) thousand; any large number
manu (*n*) bird
manuware (*adj.*) stupid; foolish
manuhiri (*n*) guest; visitor
mao (*adj.*) fine (weather)
māngai (*n*) mouth
māngere (*adj.*) lazy
mangu (*adj.*) black
maoa (*adj.*) cooked
māori (*adj.*) usual
marae (*n*) courtyard; meeting place
mārama (*adj.*) plain; clear; light (of visibility)
marama (*n.*) month, moon
mārena (*v.t.*) marry
marino (*adj.*) calm
mārire (*adj.*) quiet
    (*adv.*) gently; carefully
maroke (*adj.*) dry
mata (*n*) eye; face; edge
mātakitaki (*v.t.*) watch
mataku (*adj.*) afraid
mātao (*adj.*) cold
mataara (*adj.*) watchful; awake
matau (*adj.*) right (hand)
mātau (*v.t.*) know
mate (*adj.*) sick; dead
    (*v.i.*) suffer; die
matekai (*n*) hunger
matenga (*n*) death; sickness
matewai (*n*) thirst
mātotoru (*adj.*) thick
mātou (*pron.*) we
mātua (*adv.*) first
matua (*n*) parent
mau (*v.t.*) carry; take; bring
māu (*sing. pron.*) for you
māua (*pron.*) we two
maui (*adj.*) left (hand)
maunga (*n*) mountain

mea (*pron.*) so and so
    (*v.*) to say
meāke (*adv.*) soon
mehemea (*conj.*) if
metemea (*conj.*) as it were; as if
meneti (*n*) minute
miraka (*n*) milk
mō (*prep.*) for
moana (*n*) sea
moe (*v.i.*) sleep
moenga (*n*) marriage; sleep; bed
mōhio (*v.t.*) know; understand
mōku (*pron.*) for me
mōna (*pron.*) for him/her
moni (*n*) money
mōu (*sing. pron.*) for you
mua (*l.n.*) the front
muri (*l.n.*) behind; the rear part
mutu (*part.*) finished; left off

N

nā (*adj.*) satisfied, contented
nāhea (*l.n.*) (*past*) what time?
nāku (*pron.*) belong to me
nama (*v.t.*) borrow
nāna (*pron.*) belonging to him/her
nanahi (*l.n.*) yesterday
napō (*l.n.*) last night
nāu (*sing. pron.*) belonging to you
nāwai (*adv.*) in due course
nei (*adv.*) now; here near me
neke (*v.t.*) move
noa (*adj.*) free; common
    (*adv.*) common; without inhibition
nōhea (*adv.*) whence
nohiniho (*adj.*) small
noho (*v.i.*) sit; live; stay; remain
nōku (*pron.*) belonging to me
nōna (*pron.*) belonging to him/her
nōu (*sing. pron.*) belonging to you
nui (*adj.*) large; abundant; great

NG

ngā (*pl. art.*) the
ngahere (*n*) forest
ngākau (*n*) heart; seat of affections
ngako (*n.*) fat

ngaro (*adj.*) lost; out of sight; absent
ngāwari (*adj.*) gentle; easy; flexible
ngenge (*adj.*) weary; tired
ngoikore (*adj.*) weak

O

ō (*poss. pron. pl.*) your
o (*prep.*) of
oho (*v.i.*) awaken
okioki (*v.i.*) rest
ōku (*pron. pl.*) my
oma (*v.i.*) run
ōna (*pl. pron.*) his/her
onge (*adj.*) scarce
ope (*n*) group of people
ora (*adj.*) alive; well
oranga (*n*) life; living
ōta (*n*) order
oti (*adv.*) but
otiia (*conj.*) but (on the other hand)
otirā (*conj.*) but (at the same time)
ōu (*pl. pron.*) your
ouou (*n*) few

P

pā (*n*) fortified village
pā (*v.t.*) shut; close
pamu (*n*) farm
pahaki (*l.n.*) near distance
pahure (*v.i.*) pass by
pai (*adj.*) good, beautiful
  (*adv.*) well
  (*v.t.*) approve
pākākā (*adj.*) brown
pakaru (*adj.*) broken
  (*v.t.*) break into pieces
Pākehā (*n*) European
paki (*adj.*) fine (of weather)
pakitara (*n*) house wall
paku (*adj.*) small
pāmu (*n*) farm
pana (*v.t.*) push
pango (*adj.*) black
pāpā (*n*) father
parakuihi (*n*) breakfast
parāoa (*n*) bread, flour
paru (*n*) dirt

paruparu (*adj.*) dirty; muddy; unclean
pātai (*n*) question
pātai ki (*v.t.*) question
pātata (*adj.*) near
patu (*v.t.*) kill; strike
pau (*part*) consumed; finished
pea (*adv.*) perhaps
pēhea (*adv.*) how? of what kind?
peka (*v.i.*) turn aside
pēnā (*adv.*) like that (by you)
pēnei (*adj.*) like this
pepa (*n*) paper
pērā (*adj.*) like that (over yonder)
pia (*n*) beer
piki (*v.t.*) climb
pirau (*adj.*) rotten
pīrangi (*n*) requirement; wish
  (*v.i.*) wish, want
pito (*n*) end
pō (*n*) night
pōhēhē (*adj.*) mistaken
pokaihaka (*adj.*) confused
poke (*adj.*) dirty
popō (*v.t.*) crowd
pōrangi (*adj.*) scatty; mad
porotaka (*adj.*) round
poto (*adj.*) short
pouaka (*n*) box
pounamu (*n*) greenstone
poupou (*adj.*) steep; upright
pōuri (*adj.*) gloomy; sad; distressed
puaotanga (*n*) dawn
puare (*adj.*) open
pūhoi (*adj.*) slow
pukapuka (*n*) book; letter
puke (*n*) hill
puku (*n*) stomach
pukuriri (*adj.*) surly; annoyed
pupuri (*v.t.*) hold; retain
purei (*v.i.*) play
puta (*v.i.*) appear; come out
putiputi (*n*) flower

R

rā (*n*) day; sun
rā (*prep.*) by way of
rahi (*adj.*) large; great

rākau (*n*) wood; stick; tree
rama (*n*) lamp; electric torch
rānei (*conj.*) or
rangatira (*n*) chief; person of rank
rangi (*n*) day; heaven; song; tune
rapa; rapu (*v.t.*) seek; look for
raro (*l.n.*) bottom
raruraru (*n*) trouble
rātou (*pron.*) they
rawa (*adv.*) very
reira (*l.n.*) that place (which was previously mentioned)
reo (*n*) voice; sound, language
reta (*n*) letter
ringaringa (*n*) arm; hand
rite (*adj.*) equal; ready; like
ritenga (*n*) manner; likeness
roa (*adj.*) long; tall
roimata (*n*) tear
rongo (*v.t.*) hear; feel
rōpū (*n*) company; crowd; group
roto (*l.n.*) inside
roto (*n*) lake; pool
rua (*adj.*) two
(*n*) hole; den; pit
ruke (*v.t.*) throw away
runga (*l.n.*) top

T

tā (*v.i.*) breathe
tae (*v.i.*) arrive; achieve; reach
taha (*n*) side
tahaki (*l.n.*) aside; the shore
tahi (*adv.*) together
tahu (*v.t.*) set on fire, light
tahuri (*v.i.*) turn around; turn over; upset
tai (*n*) sea; tide
taihoa (*adv.*) by and by
tāima (*n*) time of the day (by the clock)
taimaha (*adj.*) heavy
taitama (*n*) youth
taitua (*l.n.*) far side (of something solid)
taka (*v.i.*) fall off
takai (*v.t.*) wrap

tākare (*adj.*) eager; impatient
tākaro (*v.i.*) play
take (*n*) cause; reason
takiwā (*n*) space; interval; period of time
takoto (*v.i.*) lie down
takoto kau (*adj.*) empty
tāku (*pron.*) my
tama (*n*) son
tamāhine (*n*) daughter
tamaiti (*n*) child
tamariki (*n*) children
(*adj.*) young (persons)
tāna (*pron.*) his/her
tāne (*n*) husband; human male
tāngata (*n*), men, people
tangi (*v.i.*) weep
tango (*v.t.*) take; receive
tao (*v.t.*) cook
tāone (*n*) town
taonga (*n*) riches; property
tapa (*n*) edge
tapawhā (*adj.*) square
tapoko (*v.t.*) enter
tapu (*adj.*) holy, prohibited
taratara (*adj.*) rough
tarau (*n*) trousers
tari (*n*) office, Government Department
taringa (*n*) ear
tāringa (*n*) period of waiting
tata (*adj.*) near
tatau (*n*) door
tātou (*pron.*) we
tatū (*adj.*) contented
tāu (*sing. pron.*) your
tau (*n*) year
tāua (*pron.*) we two
taua (*art.*) that (previously mentioned)
tauhou (*n*) stranger
taumaha (*adj.*) heavy
tawhiti (*adj.*) distant
(*l.n.*) distance
te (*art.*) the (*sing.*)
tēhea (*pron.*) which?

19

tēnā (*pron.*) that (by you)
tēnei (*pron.*) this
tērā (*pron.*) that (over there)
tere (*adj.*) swift; fast
tētahi (*pron.*) one; a (indef. art.)
tētahi atu (*pron.*) another
tiaki (*v.t.*) keep; protect
tihi (*n*) summit; top
tika (*adj.*) correct; just; straight
tikanga (*n*) meaning; correct way; custom
tiketike (*adj.*) high
tiki (*v.t.*) fetch
tiki (*n*) greenstone figure
tīmata (*v.t.*) begin
tinana (*n*) body
titiro (*v.i.*) look; open the eyes
tō (*sing.*) your
toe (*v.i.*) remain
toenga (*n*) remainder
tohunga (*n*) person skilled in any art
tohutohu (*v.*) advise
tōku (*sing. pron.*) my
tomo (*v.t.*) enter
tōna (*pron. sing.*) his/her
tono (*v.t.*) send; ask for
tonu (*adv.*) forward; just at; still
torutoru (*n*) few
tū (*n*) sort
tū (*v.i.*) stand
tua (*l.n.*) other side
tuarā (*n*) back
tuhituhi (*v.t.*) write
tuku (*v.t.*) let go; allow; send
tūpato (*adj.*) careful
tūpeke (*v.i.*) leap
tupuna (*n*) ancestor; grandparent
ture (*n*) law
turituri (*adj.*) noisy
tutuki (*v.i.*) be finished
tūturu (*adj.*) fixed; permanent
tuwha (*v.t.*) distribute
tūwhera (*adj.*) open

U

ū (*part*) fixed; firm
uaua (*adj.*) difficult; hard; tough

uhi (*v.t.*) cover
ui (*v.t.*) ask; question
utanga (*n*) load
utu (*v.t.*) pay; pay for; answer (*n*) price; reply; revenge; reward; return for anything

W

wā (*n*) time, place
waenga; waenganui (*l.n.*) middle
waewae (*n*) foot; leg
waha (*n*) mouth
wāhi (*n*) place; portion
wahine (*n*) woman; wife
waho (*l.n.*) outside
wai (*n*) water
wai (*inter. pron.*) who?
waiata (*v.t.*) (*n*) sing; song
waiho (*v.i.*) let be; leave alone
waka (*n*) canoe; vehicle
wareware (*v.t.*) forget
wāriu (*n*) value
wātea (*adj.*) unoccupied; free
wawe (*adv.*) soon; at once; in time
wera (*adj.*) hot (*n*) heat
wīki (*n*) week

WH

whaea (*n*) mother; aunt
whai (*v.t.*) follow
whai-taonga (*adj.*) rich
whāiti (*adj.*) narrow
whakaae (*v.t.*) agree to (*v.i.*) consent
whakaako (*v.t.*) teach
whakaara (*v.t.*) arouse; awaken
whakaatu (*v.t.*) show
whakahaere (*v.t.*) conduct; manage
whakahoki (*v.t.*) answer; cause to return
whakamanawanui (*v.i.*) be patient
whakamātau (*v.t.*) try
whakamau (*v.t.*) fix
whakamine (*v.t.*) assemble
whakamutu (*v.t.*) cease; leave off
whakanui (*v.t.*) enlarge, celebrate
whakangaro (*v.t.*) destroy
whakaoti (*v.t.*) complete

whakapono (*v.t.*) believe
whakarere (*adv.*) suddenly
whakarite (*v.t.*) perform; compare
whakatata (*v.t.*) approach
whakarongo (*v.t.*) listen
whakatika (*v.i.*) arise; stand up
whakauaua (*adj.*) difficult
whanaunga (*n*) relative
whānui (*adj.*) wide
whāngai (*v.t.*) feed

whare (*n*) house
whati (*part.*) broken
whāwhai (*adj.*) impatient
whawhati (*v.t.*) break
whea (hea) (*interrog. pron.*) where? when?
whenua (*n*) land
whero (*adj.*) red
whiriwhiri (*v.t.*) choose
whiwhi (*v.t.*) obtain

ENGLISH TO MAORI

a he; tētahi
about (approximately) tata ki
above (*prep.*) kei runga
accept (*v*) whakaaetia
accident (*n*) aituā; mate
ache (*n*) mamae
achieve (*v*) tae; whakatae
acquire (*v*) whiwhi
action (*n*) mahi
add (*v.t.*) āpiti; hono
address (*n*) kāinga
address (*v*) whaikōrero
admire (*v*) mīharo
adult (*n*) koeke; pakeke
advance (*v*) haere
advice (*n*) kupu
afar (*n*) i tawhiti
affect (*v*) pāngia
affirm (*v*) whaka-ae
afraid (*adj.*) mataku
afraid (to be) (*v.i.*) mataku
after (*prep.*) muri
afternoon (*n*) ahiahi
afterwards (*adv.*) i muri
again (*adv.*) anō
age (*n*) tau; pakeke
agony (*n*) mamae
agree (*v*) whaka-ae
agreeable (*adj.*) āhuareka
ahead (*adv.*) i mua
alas (*int.*) auē
alike (to be) (*v*) whakahua
alive (*adj.*) ora
all (*adj.*) katoa
allow (*v*) tuku
almost (*adv.*) wāhi iti
alone (*adv.*) anake
also (*adv.*) hoki
alter (*v*) **(position)** kōrure
although (*adv.*) ahakoa

altogether (*adv.*) tahi
always (*adv.*) tonu
amidst (*prep.*) i waenganui
among (*prep.*) kei roto i; i roto i
amuse (*v*) whakatākaro
amusement (*n*) mahi whakangahau
ancestor (*n*) tupuna
ancient (*adj.*) tawhito
and (*conj.*) a; mā; me
anger (*n*) riri
angry (to be) (*v*) riri
animal (*n*) kararehe
annoy (*v*) whakatoi
another (*adj.*) tētahi atu
answer (*v*) whakahoki
anus (*n*) kumu
anxious (*adj.*) āwangawanga
anxiety (*n*) mānukanuka
any (*adj.*) tētahi; ētahi
apart (*adv.*) tahaki
appear (*v*) puta
appear (*v*) **(seem) (to be)** ngia
appearance (*n*) āhua
appetite (*n*) matekai
apple (*n*) āporo
appliance (*n*) taputapu
apply (*v*) whakapātai
appoint (*v*) whakarite
approach (*v*) whakatata
approve (*v*) whakapai
argue (*v*) totohe
arise (*v*) maranga
arm (*n*) ringa
around (*prep.*) ki tētahi taha
arouse (*v*) whakaoho
arrange (*v*) whakarite
arrival (*n*) whakaekeeke
arrive (*v*) tae
as (*conj.*) i
as far as (to be) tae rawa ki

ascend (*v*) piki
ascent (*n*) pikitanga
ashamed (to be) (*v*) whakamā
ashore (to be) (*v*) kei uta
ashore (*adv.*) uta
aside (*adv.*) ki tahaki
ask (beg for) (*v*) inoi
ask (a question) (*v*) pātai (ki)
asleep (to be) (*v*) moe
assemble (*v*) hui
assemblage (*n*) hui
assembled (be) (*v*) emi
assist (*v*) āwhina
associate with (*v*) whakahoa
at (*prep.*) **(of future)** a; hei
at (place) hei; i; kei; ki
attain (*v*) tae
attempt (*v*) whakamātau
attend (*v*) whakarongo (ki)
attractive (*adj.*) ātāahua
avenue (or street) (*n*) huarahi
awake (*v*) oho
awaken (*v.t*) whakaoho
away (*adv.*) atu
awful (*adj.*) wehi

B

baby (*n*) tamaiti
bachelor (*n*) taitama
back (*adv.*) ki muri
back (*n*) tuarā
backwards (*adv.*) whakamuri
bad (*adj.*) piro; kino
bag (*n*) pēke
bake (*v*) tunu
balance (*n*) **(quantity)** toenga
bald (*adj.*) pākira
ball (*n*) pōro
bandage (*n*) (*v*) takai
bank (*n*) **(for money)** pēke
bank (*n*) **(of soil)** taha
banter (*v*) whakangako
bare (*adj.*) moremore
bargain (*v*) hoko
base (*n*) pūtake
basin (*n*) peihana
bask (*v*) **(in sun etc.)** inaina

basket (*n*) kete
bath (*n*) **(natural)** waiariki
bathe (*v*) kaukau
bay (*n*) kokorutanga
beach (*n*) one
bear (*v*) **(trouble)** manawanui
bear (*v*) **(fruit)** hua
bear (*v*) **(carry)** kawe
beard (*n*) pāhau
beat (*v*) **(in, of rain)** hawhe
beat (*v*) taupatupatu
beaten (*adj.*) pīti
beautiful (*adj.*) ātāahua
because (*conj.*) nō te mea; hoki
beckon (*v*) pōwhiri
bed (*v*) moenga
bedroom (*v*) rūma moe
beer (*v*) pia
begin (*v*) tīmata
beginning (*n*) tīmatanga
behind (*prep.*) i muri i
believe (*v*) whakapono
belonging to (*vbl. sb.*) a; nō
below (*prep.*) ki raro i
benzine (*n*) pēnehini
beside (*prep.*) i teitaha
besides (*prep.*) hāunga
best (*adj.*) tino pai
better (*adj.*) pai atu
between (*prep.*) ki waenganui
bible (*n*) paipera
big (*adj.*) nui, rahi
bill (*n*) **(commerce)** kaute
billiards (*n*) piriota
bird (*n*) manu
biscuit (*n*) pīhikete
bit (*n*) **(portion)** maramara
black (*adj.*) mangu
blanket (*n*) paraikete
bleed (*v*) toto
bless (*v*) whakapai
block (*n*) **(of land)** poraka
blood (*n*) toto
blossom (*n*) pua
blue (*adj.*) purū
boast (*v*) whakaputa

boat (*n*) waka
body (*n*) tinana
bold (*adj.*) toa
book (*n*) pukapuka
boot (*n*) pūtu
border (*n*) (**land**) rohe
border (*n*) (**cloth**) remu
born (*v*) (**to be**) whānau
bosom (*n*) uma
boss (*n*) pāhi
bottle (*n*) pātara, pounamu
bottom (*n*) raro
boundary (*n*) rāina
bowl (*n*) kumete
box (*n*) pouaka
boy (*n*) taitama
branch (*n*) manga
brand (*n*) parani
bread (*n*) parāoa
break (*v*) (**into pieces**) tātā, wāhi
breakfast (*n*) parakuihi
breath (*n*) manawa
breathe (*v*) whakaeaea
breeze (*n*) hau
bridge (*n*) piriti
bright (*adj.*) (**shining**) kanapu
bright (*adj.*) (**clever**) mūrere
bring (*v*) mauria
broad (*adj.*) whānui
broken (*adj.*) pakaru
brown (*adj.*) parāone
build (*v*) hanga
builder (*n*) kaihanga
bundle (*n*) paihere
burn (*v*) ngiha
bus (*n*) pahi
bush (*n*) ngahere
busy (*adj.*) raru
butcher (*n*) pūtia
butter (*n*) pata
button (*n*) pātene
buy (*v*) hoko
buyer (*n*) kaihoko

C

cake (*n*) keke
calculate (*v*) tatau
calendar (*n*) maramataka
calico (*n*) kareko
call (*v*) karanga
calm (*adj.*) marino
camera (*n*) kāmera
capable (*adj.*) kakama
car (*n*) motokā
card (*n*) kāri
careful (*adj.*) tūpato
careless (*adj.*) koretake
carpet (*n*) kāpeti
carry (*v*) kawe
cart (*n*) kāta
carve (*v*) whakairo
case (*n*) kēhi
cat (*n*) ngeru; poti
catch (*v*) hopu
cause (*v*) mea
cease (*v*) mutu
cemetery (*n*) urupā
centre (*n*) waenganui
cent (*n.*) henetii
certificate (*n*) tiwhikete
chair (*n*) tūru
change (*v*) whakaputa kē
chant (*n*) (*v*) waiata
chatter (*v*) (*n*) kōrerorero (rero)
cheerful (*adj.*) ngahau
chief (*n*) ariki
child (*n*) tamaiti
children (*n*) tamariki
chocolate (*n*) tiakarete
choose (*v*) whiriwhiri
church (*n*) hāhi
clap (*v*) pakipaki
clean (*adj.*) mā
cleanse (*v*) horoi
clear (*adj.*) ūtea
clear (*v*) tahi
clearing (*n*) (**in bush**) waerenga
clever (*adj.*) mūrere
climb (*v*) piki
clock (*n*) karaka
close (*adj.*) tata
close (*v*) kopi
clothe (*v*) kākahu

clothing (*n*) kākahu
cloud (*n*) kapua
cloudy (*adj.*) kōngū
clumsy (*adj.*) pakihawa
coast (*n*) takutai
coat (*n*) koti
cold (*adj.*) makariri
cold (*n*) tarutawhiti
come (*v*) (**hither**) haere mai
companion (*n*) hoa
compare (*v*) whakarite
complain (*v*) amuamu
comprehend (*v*) mōhio
concert (*n*) kōnohete
conclusion (**ending**) (*n*) mutunga
conduct (*v*) ārahi
consent (*v*) whakaae
consider (*v*) whakaaro
constable (*n*) pirīhimana
consume (*v*) whakapau
converse (*v*) kōrerorero
cook (*v*) tao
cook (*n*) kuki
cool (*adj.*) hauhau
cost (*n*) utu
corner (*n*) kokonga
country (*n*) whenua
court (*n*) (**law**) kōti
creased (*adj.*) kopakopa
crossroad (*n*) ara rīpeka
crowd (*v*) inaki
crowd (*n*) huihuinga
cup (*n*) kapu
custom (*n*) tikanga

D

daily (*adj.*) i tēnei rā, i tēnei rā
dam (*n*) matatara
dance (*n*) (*v*) haka
dark (*adj.*) pōuri
dawn (*n*) atapō
day (*n*) rā; rangi; ao
daylight (*n*) awatea
dead (*adj.*) mate
dear (**expensive**) (*adj.*) utu nui
debt (*n*) nama
deliver (*v*) whakaora

demand (*v*) tono
depart (*v*) haere atu
descend (*v*) heke
describe (*v*) whakaatu i te āhua
desire (*v*) wawata
desire (*n*) hia
detain (*v*) pupuri
die (*v*) mate
difficult (*adj.*) uaua
direct (**indicate**) (*v*) tohutohu
direct (*adj.*) tika
dirt (*n*) paru
discomfort (*n*) hūhī
discover (*v*) kite
discuss (*v*) whiriwhiri
dish (*n*) rīhi
do (*v*) mea, mahi
doctor (*n*) tākuta
dollar (*n.*) tara
donation (*n*) koha
door (*n*) kuaha
dress (*n*) (*v*) kākahu
drive (*v*) (**a car etc.**) taraiwa
dust (*n*) puehu
dwell (*v*) noho
dwelling (*n*) whare

E

ear (*n*) taringa
early (*adj.*) moata
earth (*n*) ao
east (*n*) rāwhiti
eat (*v*) kai
emigrate (*v*) heke
end (*n*) (**finishing**) mutunga
ended (*adj.*) mutu
end (*n*) (**of a thing**) pito
England (*n*) Ingarangi
Englishman (*n*) Ingarihi
enough (*adv.*) heoi; ka nui
enquire (*v*) ui
enter (*v*) tomo
entertain (*v*) whakangahau
entertainment (*n*) mahi whakangahau
entrance (*n*) tomokanga
erect (*v*) whakatū

25

establish (*v*) whakanoho
evening (*v*) ahiahi
ever (*adv.*) tonu
every (*adj.*) katoa
example (*n*) tauira
excellent (*adj.*) rawe
explain (*v*) whakamārama
explore (*v*) toro
exposed (*adj.*) puare
eye (*n*) kanohi, karu, whatu

F

face (*n*) mata
factory (*n*) wheketere
fair (colouring) (*n*) kiritea
fair (climate) (*n*) paki
fall (*v*) hinga
family (*n*) whānau
farm (*n*) pāmu
fast (*adj.*) **(of speed)** tere
fat (*adj.*) mōmona
father (*n*) pāpā
fatigued (*adj.*) ngenge
feast (*n*) hākari

feed (*v*) whāngai
feel (*v*) **(with hands)** whāwhā
feel (*v*) **(mentally)** rongo
female (animal) (*n*) uwha
female (human) (*n*) wahine
fetch (*v*) tiki
field (*n*) māra
find (*v*) kite
fine (*adj.*) **(climate)** paki
finish (use up) (*v*) whakapau
finished (*adj.*) **(used up)** pau
fish (*v*) **(angling)** hī
fish (*n*) ika
fix (*v*) whakapai
flat (*adj.*) papatahi
flower (*n*) putiputi
fly (*v*) rere
follow (*v*) aru, whai
food (*n*) kai
foot (*n*) waewae
football (*n*) hutupōro
foreigner (*n*) Pākehā; tauiwi
forest (*n*) ngahere

forget (*v*) wareware
France (*n*) Wīwī
French (**man**) (**woman**) Wīwī
free (*adj.*) wātea
fresh (*adj.*) (**of fruit**) kaimata
friend (*n*) hoa
front (*n*) mua
fruit (*n*) hua
full (**to be**) (*v*) (*also adj.*) kī
further (*adv.*) ki kō atu

G

gale (*n*) āwhā
garden (*n*) māra
garment (*n*) kākahu
gasoline (*n*) penehīni
gate (*n*) kēti
gateway (*n*) kūwaha
gather (*v*) (**people**) huihui
generous (*adj.*) atawhai
gentle (*adj.*) mārire
genuine (*adj.*) tupu
Germany (*n*) Tiamana
gift (*n*) koha
girdle (*n*) whītiki
girl (*n*) kōtiro
give (**to**; **away**) (*v*) hōmai; hoatu
glad (*adj.*) hari
glass (*n*) karāhe
go (*v*) haere atu
god (*n*) atua
gold (*adj.*) (*n*) kōura
gone (**to be**) (*v*) riro
gone (**finished**) (*adj.*) pau
good (*adj.*) pai
goods (*n*) taonga
got (*v*) riro (part.)
grasp (*v*) tango
grass (*n*) karāihe
great (*adj.*) nui
greedy (*adj.*) kaihoro
green (**colouring**) (*adj.*) kākāriki
green (**fruit**) (*n*) ota
greenstone (*n*) pounamu
greet (*v*) mihi
grief (*n*) pōuri
ground (*n*) whenua

grumble (*v*) amuamu
guard (*v*) tiaki
guest (*n*) manuhiri
guide (*n*) kaiārahi
guide (*v*) ārahi

H

habit (*n*) ritenga
hair (**of body**) huruhuru
hair (**of head**) makawe
half (*n*) hāwhe
halfcaste (*n*) hāwhe kāehe
halt (*v*) tū
hand (*n*) ringaringa
handful (*n*) kapunga
handle (*v*) whāwhā
happen (*v*) tūpono
hard (*adj.*) mārō
harm (*n*) kino
hasten (*v*) hohoro
hat (*n*) pōtae
haul (*v*) kume
head (*n*) mātenga
headache (*n*) ānini
heal (*v*) whakaora
healed (*adj.*) ora
health (*n*) ora
hear (*v*) rongo
heat (*n*) wera
heaven (*n*) rangi
heavy (*adj.*) taimaha
height (*n*) tiketike
help (*v*) āwhina
hide (*v*) ngaro
high (*adj.*) tiketike
hill (*n*) puke
hold (*v*) pupuri
holiday (*n*) hararei
holy (*adj.*) tapu
home (*n*) kāinga
hospital (*n*) hōhipera
host (*n*) (**in a house etc.**) tangata whenua
hot (*adj.*) (**temperature**) wera; kakā
hot (*adj.*) (**to palate**) pūhahana
hotel (*n*) hōtēra
hour (*n*) hāora

house (*n*) whare
how (*adv.*) pēwhea
hungry (*adj.*) **hunger** (*n*) mate kai; hiakai
hurry (*v*) pōrangi
hurt (*v*) ngau
hurt (to be) (*v*) whara
husband (*n*) tāne

I

I (oneself) (*pron.*) ahau; au
icecream (*n*) aihikirīmi
idle (*adj.*) māngere
ill, to be (*v*) mate
immediately (*adv.*) āianei tonu
impatient (*adj.*) pōrangi
important (*adj.*) nui
inch (*n*) inihi
increase (*v*) nui haere
India (*n*) Inia
industrious (*adj.*) mamahi
influenza (*n*) rewharewha
inform (*v*) whakaatu
inhabit (*v*) noho
injure; be injured (*v*) tūkino
injury (*n*) tūkinotanga
ink (*n*) mangumangu
inland (*n*) uta
inquire (*v*) pātai
inside (*adv.*) roto
insolent (*adj.*) toro
inspect (*v*) mātakitaki
inspector (*n*) kaitirotiro
instruct (*v*) ako
insult (*v*) kanga
intelligent (*adj.*) mōhio
intercourse (sexual) (*v*) mahimahi
interest (money) (*n*) itarete
interior (*adj.*) roto
interior (inland) (*n*) uta
interpret (*v*) whakamāori
interpreter (*n*) kaiwhakamāori
interrupt (*v*) aruaru
intoxicated (*adj.*) haurangi
Irish (*adj.*) (*n*) Airihi
iron (*n*) rino
island (*n*) motu

J

jail (*n*) whare herehere
jersey (*n*) poraka
join (*v*) hono
journey (*v*) haerenga
jump (*v*) peke

K

keep (*v*) tiaki
keepsake (*n*) manatunga
kind (be) (*v*) (*adj.*) atawhai
kiss (*n*) (*v*) kihi
kitchen (*n*) kīhini
kneel (*n*) tūturi
know (*v*) mōhio
knowledge (*n*) mātauranga

L

labour (*n*) (*v*) mahi
lady (*n*) wahine rangatira
lake (*n*) roto
lamp (*n*) rama
land (*n*) whenua
land (*v*) tau
language (*n*) reo
large (*adj.*) nui
last (*v*) piwai
last (*n*) **(of things)** toenga
late (*adj.*) tōmuri
late (to be) (*v*) akuaku
laugh (*v*) kata
law (*n*) ture
lazy (*adj.*) māngere
lead (*v*) ārahi
leader (*n*) kaiārahi
leaf (*n*) rau
lean (*v*) wharara
learn (*v*) ako
learner (*n*) akonga
leather (*n*) rera
leave; be left (*v*) waiho
leg (*n*) waewae
legend (*n*) kōrero tupuna
length (*n*) roa
let go (*v*) tuku
let (lease) (*v*) rīhi
letter (*n*) reta
licence (*n*) raihana

lie down (*v*) takoto
life (*n*) ora
light (visibility) (*adj.*) mārama
light (weight) (*adj.*) māmā
light (*v*) tahu
light (*n*) raiti
like (*adj.*) rite
like (*v*) āhuareka
likeness (*n*) āhua
likewise (*adv.*) hoki
liquid (*n*) wai
listen (*v*) whakarongo
little (*adj.*) iti
live (*v*) noho
look (at) (*v*) titiro (ki)
look (*v*) **(search)** rapu
lost (*adj.*) ngaro
love (*adj.*) (*v*) aroha
lucky (*adj.*) waimarie
lunch (*n*) tina

M

machine (*n*) mīhini
mad (*adj.*) pōrangi
mail (*n*) mēra
mainland (*n*) tuawhenua
male (*n*) **(human)** tāne
man (*n*) tangata
manage (be able) (*v*) tae
manner (*n*) ritenga
many (*adj.*) tini, maha
map (*n*) mapi
marry (*v*) mārena
mate (*n*) hoa
me (*pron.*) ahau
meaning (*n*) tikanga
measure (*v*) tatai
medicine (*n*) rongoā
meet (*v*) tūtaki
meeting (*n*) hui
mend (*v*) tapi
merchandise (*v*) taonga
merry (*adj.*) koa
message (*n*) kupu
messenger (*n*) karere
method (*n*) tikanga
middle (*adj.*) waenganui

migrate (*v*); **migration** (*n*) heke
mild (*adj.*) mahaki
mile (*n*) māero
milk (*n*) miraka
mine (*pron.*) nāku; nōku
minute (*n*) meneti
mirror (*n*) mira
misfortune (*n*) aituā
mist (*n*) kohu
moist (*adj.*) mākūku
money (*n*) moni
moon (*n*) marama
moonlight (*n*) atarau
morsel (*n*) maramara
mother (*n*) whaea, māmā
motor car (*n*) motokā
mountain (*n*) maunga
mouth (*n*) waha
move (about) (*v*) korikori
move (away) (*v*) hoatu
move (in a certain direction) (*v*) neke
much (*adj.*) nui
my (*pron.*) taku

N

naked (*adj.*) pakiwhara
name (*n*) ingoa
name (*v*) tapa
nation (*n*) iwi
near (*adj.*) tata
nevertheless (*adv.*) ahakoa
new (*adj.*) hou
news (*n*) kōrero (o te wā)
nice (*adj.*) reka
night (*n*) pō
no (*adv.*) kāhore
noise (*n*) turituri
nose (*n*) ihu
not yet kāhore anō
now (*adv.*) āianei
nuisance (*n*) taitāhae
number (*n*) nama
numerous (*adj.*) tini
nurse (*n*) nēhi

O

obedient (*adj.*) ngawari
obey (*v*) rongo
object (*n*) mea
observe (*v*) titiro
obtain (*v*) whiwhi
occupation (*n*) mahi
ocean (*n*) moana
offence (*n*) hara
office (*n*) tari
old (*adj.*) (**things**) tawhito
old (*adj.*) (**people**) koroheke
only (*adv.*) anake
open (*adj.*) puare
open (*v*) huakina
opinion (*n*) whakaaro
opposite (*adj.*) anga
orange (*adj.*) (*n*) ārani
order (*v*) whakahau
order (**put in**) whakapai
out (*adv.*) (**outside**) waho
over (*prep.*) ki runga i

P

pack (*n*) kawenga
pack (*v*) takai
paddock (*n*) pātiki
paid (*adj.*) ea
pain (*n*) mamae
pair (*n*) pūrua
palatable (*adj.*) reka
pale (*adj.*) mā
pants (*n*) tarau
paper (*n*) pepa
parent (*n*) matua
part; portion (*n*) wāhi
participate (*v*) uru
party (of people) (*n*) rōpū
pass by (*v*) pahure
pass through (*v*) puta
passage (*n*) ara
past (*n*) pāhi
path (*n*) ara
pause (*v*) okioki
pay (*v*)**; payment** (*n*) utu
peep (*v*) titiro
people (*n*) iwi

perceive (*v*) kite
perfect (*adj.*) pai rawa atu
perhaps (*adv.*) pea
permit (*v*) tuku
person (*n*) tangata
photograph (*n*) whakaahua
photograph (*v*) tango whakaal
picnic (*n*) pikiniki
place (*n*) wāhi
plan (*n*) tikanga
play (*v*) purei
pleasant (*adj.*) āhuareka
plentiful (*adj.*) tini
point out (*v*) tuhi
policeman (*n*) pirihimana
poor (*adj.*) rawakore
possess (*v*) whai
possessions (*n*) taonga
post office (*n*) poutāpeta
power (*n*) mana
practice (*n*) ritenga
pray (*v*) inoi
prepare (*v*) takatū
present (gift) (*n*) koha
presently (*adv.*) ākuanei
pretty (*adj.*) ātaahua
price (*n*) utu
proceed (*v*) haere
proper (*adj.*) tika
prove (*v*) whakamātau
purchase (*v*) hoko mai
purse (*n*) pāhi

Q

quantity (*n*) nui
quarrel (*v*) pakanga
quarter (*n*) koata
question (*v*) ui (ki) pātai
quick (*adj.*) hohoro; tere
quiet (*adj.*) mārie

R

races (horses) (*n*) purei hōiho
radio (*n*) waerehe; reo irirang
railway (*n*) rerewe
rain (*n*) (*v*) ua
raise (*v*) hāpai
random (*adj.*) noa

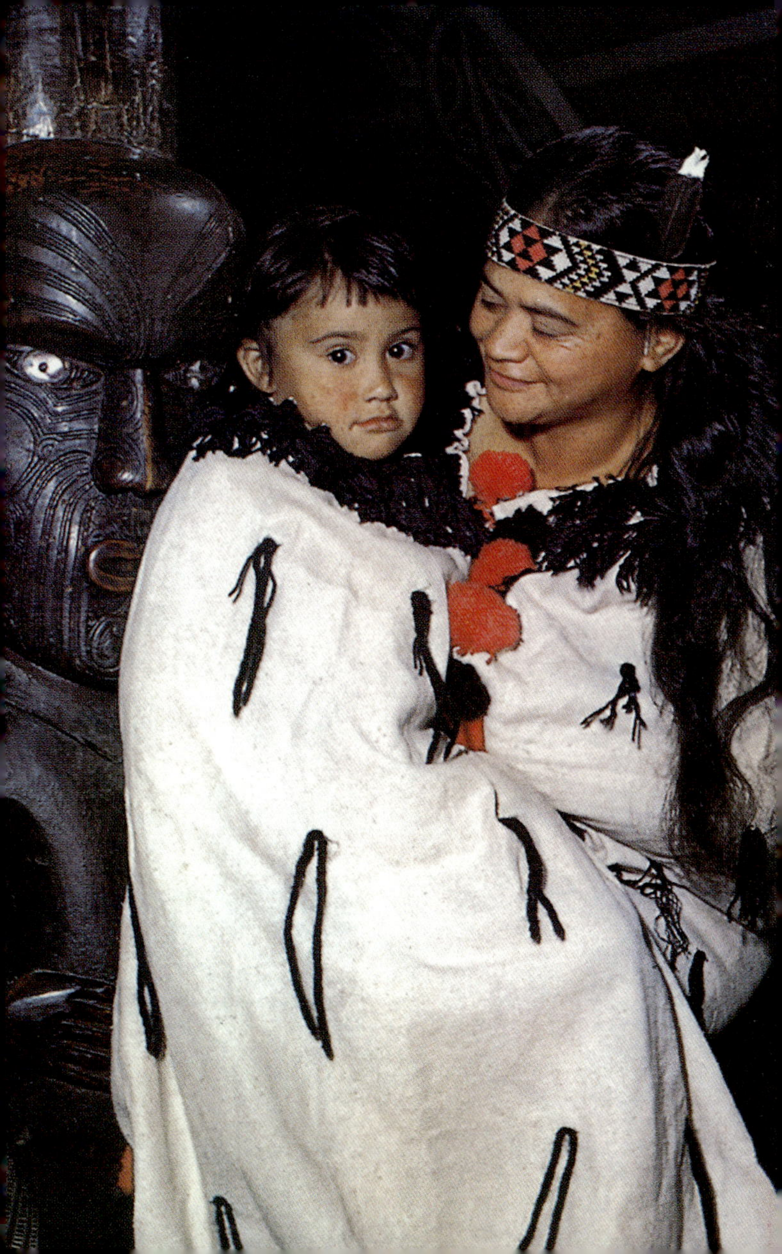

rapid (*adj.*) tere
rather (*adv.*) ēngari
read (*v*) kōrero pukapuka
ready (*adj.*) rite
rear (*n*) muri
reason (*n*) tikanga
receive (*v*) tango
recent (*adj.*) hou
recently (*adv.*) inākuarā
recognise (*v*) mōhio
red (*adj.*) whero
refresh (*v*) whakangā
refreshment (*n*) ora
refuse (*v*) whakakāhore
rejoice (*v*) hari
religion (*n*) hāhi
remain (*v*) noho
remark (*n*) kupu
remark (*v*) kōrero
remedy (*n*) rongoā
reply (*v*) whakahoki
request (*v*) (*n*) inoi
residence (*n*) whare
rest (*v*) okioki
resting place (*n*) okiokinga
return (*v.t.*) whakahoki
return (*v.i.*) hoki
rich (*adj.*) whai taonga
right (*adj.*) (**correct**) tika
right hand (*n*) ringa matau
ripe (*adj.*) maoa
road (*n*) huarahi
room (*n*) rūma
rotten (*adj.*) pirau
round (*adj.*) porotaka
run (*v*) (*n*) (**-er**) oma
rush (*v*) huaki
Russia (*n*) Rūhia
sack (*n*) pēke
sacred (*adj.*) tapu
sad (*adj.*) pōuri
safe (*adj.*); **safety** (*n*) ora
sale (*n*) hokohoko
sand (*n*) onepū
satisfied (*adj.*) mākona
save (*v*) whakaora

say (*v*) kōrero
scare (*v*) whakawehi
scent (*n*) tiare
school (*n*) kura
Scotsman (*n*) Kōtimana
scream (*v*) tiwē
sea (*n*) tai
search (*v*) kimi
season (*n*) wā
secret (*adj.*) puku
seek (*v*) rapu
seize (*v*) hopu
select (*v*) whiriwhiri
sell (*v*) hoko
send (*v*) ngare
settle (*v*) tatū
sew (*v*) tuitui
shame (*n*) whakamā
she (*pron.*) ia
ship (*n*) kaipuke
shore (*n*) takutai
short (*adj.*) poto
shout (*v*) karanga
show (*v*) whakakite
shut; be shut (*v*) kati
sick (*adj.*) māuiui
sickness (*n*) māuiuitanga
side (*n*) taha
sight (*v*) kite
sight (*n*) kitenga
sign (*n*) (*v*) tohu
silent, be (*v*) hāngū
silly (*adj.*) rorirori
sin (*n*) hara
sing (*v*); **song** (*n*) waiata
single (*adj.*) tapatahi
sit (*v*) noho
size (*n*) nui
skill (*n*); **skilful** (*adj.*) mātau
skin (*n*) kiri
sky (*n*) rangi
slap (*v*) papaki
sleep (*v*) moe
slow (*adj.*) roa
small (*adj.*) iti
smell (*v*) rongo**

smile (*v*) menemene ngā pāpāringa
smoke (**pipe etc.**) (*v*) kai paipa
smooth (*adj.*) māeneene
soak (*v*) kōpiro
soap (*n*) hopi
soft (*adj.*) ngāwari
soil (*n*) oneone
solid (*adj.*) pakeke
son (*n*) tama
soon (*adv.*) aianei
sore (*adj.*) mamae
speech (*n*) reo
speech (*n*); **oration** (*n*) whaikōrero
speed (*n*) tere
stand (*v*) tū
start (*v*) (**begin**) tīmata
starve (*v*) mate i te kai (lit: "die for food")
station (*n*) teihana
stay (*v*) noho
step (*v*) (*n*) hiko
stick (*n*) rākau
stink (*v*) piro
stomach (*n*) puku
stop (*v*) (**halt**) tū
stop (*v*) (**restrain**) pupuri
stop (*v*) (**prevent**) ārai
store (**shop**) (*n*) toa
storm (*n*) tūpuhi
straight (*adj.*) tika
stranger (*n*) tauhou
street (*n*) huarahi
strength (*n*) kaha
strike (*v*) (**hit**) patu
strive (*v*) tohe
strong (*adj.*) kaha
subject (*n*) take
suddenly (*adv.*) whakarere
suit (*n*) hūtu
suitable (*adj.*) rawe
summer (*n*) raumati
sun (*n*) rā
supper (*n*) hapa
support (*v*) whakawhirinaki
suppose (*v*) whakaaro
sure, be (*v*) mōhio tonu

surprise (*v*) (**emotion**) mīharo
sweet (*adj.*) reka
swift (*adj.*) hohoro
swim (*v*) kauhoe

T

table (*n*) tēpu
take (*v*) tango
talk (*v*) (*n*) kōrero
tall (*adj.*) teitei
taste (*n*) (*v*) rongo
tax (*n*) take
taxi (*n*) tākihi
teach (*v*) whakaako
teacher (*n*) māhita
telegram (*n*) waea
telephone (*n*) (*v*) whounu; rīngi
tell (*v*) whakaatu
tender (*adj.*) ngāwari
terrible (*adj.*) mataku
thank (*v*) whakapai
thank you! ka pai!
the ngā
therefore (*conj.*) koia
these (*pron.*) ēnei
thief (*n*) tāhae
thin (*adj.*) rahirahi
thing (*n*) mea
think (*v*) mahara
thirst (*n*) (**-y**) (*adj.*) hiainu
this (*pron.*) tēnei
thoroughly (*adv.*) mārire
those (*pron.*) (**by you**) ēnā (over there) ērā
thought (*n*) mahara
throw (*v*) panga
thus (*adv.*) pēnei
ticket (*n*) tīkiti
tide (*n*) tai
tight (*adj.*) kikī
time (*n*) tāima
timid (*adj.*) wehi
tired (*adj.*) ngenge
together (*adv.*) ngātahi
toil (*v*) (*n*) mahi
too (*adv.*) hoki
torch (*n*) rama

33

total (*n*) te katoa
tourist (*n*) tūruhi
town (*n*) tāone
track (*n*) ara
tradition (*n*) hītori
train (*n*) tereina
translate (*v*) whakamāori
travel (*v*) takihaere
traveller (*n*) tangata haere
tree (*n*) rākau
tribe (*n*) iwi
trouble (*n*) aituā
trousers (*n*) tarau
truck (*n*) taraka
true (*adj.*) pono
trust (*v*) whakapono
truth (*n*) pono
try (*v*) whakamātau
tune (*n*) rangi
turn (*v*) tahuri
twice (*adv.*) tuarua

U

ugly (*adj.*) āhua kino
uncertain (*adj.*) rangirua
uncooked (*adj.*) ota
under (*prep.*) kei raro
understand (*v*) mātau
unfortunate (*adj.*) aituā
unless (*conj.*) ki te kore .. e
unpaid (*adj.*) tārewa
unpalatable (*adj.*) kawa
unsteady (*adj.*) tatutatu
until (*prep.*) apanoa
upon (*prep.*) ki runga ki
upset, to be (*v*) tahuri
urge (*v*) akiaki
use (*v*) tangotango

V

vacant (*adj.*) wātea
valley (*n*) awaawa
value (*n*) wāriu
variable (*adj.*) haurokuroku
very (*adv.*) tino
view (*n*) tirohanga
village (*n*) kāinga
violent (*adj.*) taikaha

visit (*v*) whakatau
visitor (*n*) manuhiri
voice (*n*) reo

wages (*n*) utu
waist (*n*) hope
wait (*v*) tatari
wake (*v.i.*) *v.t.*) ara; whakaara
walk (*v*) haere-a-waewae
wallet (*n*) pāhi
wander (*v*) kotiti haere
want (*v*) pīrangi
warm (*adj.*) (*v*) werawera; whakawerawera
warrior (*n*) toa
wash (*v*) horoi
watch (*n*) wati
watch (*v*) mataki
water (*n*) (**fresh**) (**salt**) wai (māori) (tai)
way (*n*) (**path**) ara
way (*n*) (**manner**) ritenga
weak (*adj.*) (**of things**) ngoikore
weak (*adj.*) (**mentally etc.**) hauarea
wealth (*n*) taonga
weariness (*n*) ngenge
wed (*v*) mārena
week (*n*) wiki
weight (*n*) taimaha
well (*adj.*) ora
west (*n*) hauāuru
wet (*adj.*) (*n*) mākū
what? (*interr.*) aha?
when? (*interr.*) ahea?
when? (*adv.*) ana?
where? (*adv.*) hea?
which? (*pron.*) tēhea?
white (*adj.*) mā
who? (*pron.*) wai?
whole (*adj.*) katoa
whose? (*pron.*) nā (nō) wai?
why? (*adv.*) he aha?
wicked (*adj.*) kino
wide (*adj.*) whānui
widow (*n*) pouaru
wife (*n*) wahine

wild (*adj.*) māka
will (*n*) wira
wind (*n*) hau
wine (*n*) wāina
winter (*n*) makariri
wisdom (*n*) mātauranga
wish (*n*) (*v*) hiahia
woman (*n*) wahine
wonder (*v*) mīharo
wonderful (*adj.*) whakamīharo
wood (*n*) rākau
wool (*n*) wūru
word (*n*) kupu
work (*n*) mahi
world (*n*) ao
worry (*v*) māharahara
worship (*v*) (*n*) karakia

wrap up (*v*) takai
write (*v*) tuhituhi
wrong (*adj.*) (*n*) hē

Y

yard (*n*) (**enclosure**) marae
yard (*n*) (**distance**) iāri
year (*n*) tau
yellow (*adj.*) pungapunga
yes (*adv.*) ae
yet (*conj.*) anō
yonder (*adv.*) ki ko
you (*pron*) (*sing.*) (*plural*) koe, korua, koutou
youth (*n*) taitama

Z

zeal (*n*) uaua
zigzag (*adj.*) kopikopiko

CONVERSATIONAL PHRASES

We now give a number of conversational phrases which the visitor can memorise and use on appropriate occasions. Although the basic sentences and phrases are in the vicinity of 250 in number, with a little ingenuity this number can be almost doubled by substituting words from the vocabulary for key words in the sentences. Where substitution is feasible the word is shown in italics in both the English and Maori versions of the sentence. For example: We are going back *home*. E hoki ana tatou ki *te kainga*. Reference to the vocabulary will suggest substitutes for "home". For example "pāmu" (farm) can be used so that the sentence reads: E hoki ana tatou ki te pāmu—we are going back to the farm. In some cases several alternatives are suggested.

For example:

I am going *home/to the hotel/to my friend's house*—E hoki ana ahau ki *toku kainga/te hotera/te kainga o taku hoa*. This means that the sentence can be written as:

E hoki ana ahau ki toku kainga (going home) *or*

E hoki ana ahau ki te hotera (going to the hotel) *or*

E hoki ana ahau ki te kainga o taku hoa (going to the house of my friend).

In many cases the suggested substitution is the pronoun (I, she, he etc.) and here a word of caution is necessary to ensure that the correct form of the pronoun is used. Here are the principal forms of the Maori pronoun. *It must be noted that unlike English (which has only a singular and plural form), Maori has three forms or numbers.* These are singular (one), dual (two people), plural (more than two).

Singular	*Dual*	*Plural*
ahau or *au* (I, me)	*taua* (we, us—you and I)	*tatou* (we, us—you and I)
	maua (we, us—he and I)	*matou* (we, us—they and I)
Koe (you)	*korua* (you two)	*koutou* (you—all of you)
Ia (he, she, him, her)	*raua* (they, them two)	*ratou* (they, them, all of them)

Read also the introductory remarks to the vocabulary on page 11 and you should know enough basic Maori grammar to start constructing sentences of your own around the models given in the following pages.

GREETINGS; PERSONAL HEALTH; THANKS; COURTESY PHRASES

Hullo (to one other person)	Tēnā koe.
(to two others)	Tēnā kōrua.
(to many)	Tēnā koutou.
How are you? (to one/to two/to many)	Kei te pehea *koe/korua/koutou*.
Very well, thank you	Ka nui te pai.
Hello	Kia ora.*
What is your name?	Ko wai tou ingoa?
My name is *Charles*.	Ko *Taare* taku ingoa.
How old are you?	Ka hia ou tau?
Who are your parents?	Ko wai ou matua?
Where do you live?	Kei whea tou kainga tuturu?
Goodbye (from the one going to the person staying!	E noho ra.
(from the person staying to the one going!	Haere ra.
I'm fine/good/o.k.	Kei te pai.
How are they all at home?	Kei te pewhea nga tangata o te kainga?
They are well.	Kei te pai katoa.
What's wrong with *you*?	He aha *tou* mate?
I feel ill.	Ka nui taku hiahia ruaki.
I've a cold.	He rewharewha toku.
What tribe do you belong to?	He aha tou hapu?
Will *you* accept this?	E pai ranei *koe* ki te tango i tenei?
You're welcome to it.	E pai ana; mauria.
You are very kind.	Ka nui to aroha.
Thank you for your kindness.	Ka whakapai ahau ki a koe mo tau atawhai.
Excellent!	Pai rawa atu!
What a pleasure.	Katahi te koa.
How nice.	Ano te pai.
I'm glad.	E koa ana ahau.
I wish *you* luck.	Kia ora *koe*.
I am very pleased with it.	E ahuareka ana ahau ki tena.
I can't help that.	E taea hoki a ahau te aha.
He's/She's my friend (best friend!)	Ko ia taku hoa (pai rawa atu).
Please sit down.	E noho ki raro.
I am sorry to trouble *you*.	E pouri ana ahau mo taku whakararuraru i a *koe*.

*(Tena koe is a more formal greeting on first aquaintance or to someone you have not seen for a time. It is the sort of greeting often accompanied by a handshake. "Kia ora" is more informal — the greeting to use to your workmates whom you see each day, for example.)

EATING AND DRINKING

The meal is ready.	Kua reri nga kai.
This food is good.	Ka pai te kai.
I'm hungry.	E hia kai ana *ahau*.
I'm thirsty.	E hia inu ana *ahau*.
I can't eat.	E kore *ahau* e kaha ki te kai.
We are very hungry.	Kei te hemo kai matou.
What will you have to eat?	He aha te kai e hiahia ana koe?
Give me something to eat.	Homai etahi kai maku.
I have eaten enough.	Kua makona *ahau*.
Eat *quickly/slowly*.	Kia *tere/roa* te kai.
The water is cold.	Ka makariri te wai.
Give me something to drink.	Homai etahi inu maku.
Let me have some *beer/water*.	Homai he *pia/wai* maku.

OF WORK AND DOING THINGS

What do *you* want done?	He aha te mahi e mea nei *koutou* kia mahia?
What shall *we* do?	Me pewhea ra *tatou*?
What do you want to do?	He aha tau e hiahia ana kia meatia?
What is there to be done?	E taea koia te pewhea?
I don't know what to do.	Kahore i te kitea e au he tikanga maku.
That'll do.	Kati rawa.
That's enough for today.	Kati te mahi mo tenei ra.
I cannot do it now.	E kore e taea e ahau inaianei.
What is he doing? (What does he do?)	He aha tana mahi?
What are *you* doing?	I te aha *koe*?
He is working.	Kei te mahi ia.
How is your work going.	E pehea ana te mahi.
What are we going to do now?	E aha ana tatou inaianei?
We are going back *home*.	E hoki ana tatou ki *te kainga*.
What's he good for?	He aha tona pai?
He's lazy.	He tangata mangere ia.
She's lazy.	He wahine mangere ia.

COMING AND GOING; SEEKING DIRECTIONS

Let's go (the two of us) (more than two).	Me haere tahi (taua) (tatou).
Which way shall *we* go?	Me tehea huarahi *tatou* haere ai?
Where are *you* going?	E aha ana *koutou* kohea?
I (you) will go.	Ka haere ahau (koe).
When are *you* going?	A whea *koe* haere ai?
Go straight ahead.	Haere tika tonu atu.
Turn right/left.	Me peka ki to ringa matau/maui.
I am going home/to the hotel/to my friend's house/to John's house.	E hoki ana ahau ki *toku kainga/te hotera/te kainga o taku hoa/te whare o Hoani*.
Where shall we (more than two) go?	Me aha tatou ki hea?
At last *he* has gone.	Katahi *ia* ka riro.
Don't go.	Kaua e haere.
Go!	Haere atu!
Climb up here.	Piki mai.
Come here.	Haere mai.
Go back!	Hoki!
They went there.	I haere ratou ki reira.
Go carefully.	Kia tupato te haere.
Where did *you* come from?	I haere mai *koe* i hea?
I have come from home.	I haere mai ahau i toku kainga.
This is the *second time* I have come here.	Ko *te rua* tenei o aku haerenga mai.
Come with me.	Hoki mai i ahau.
I had better go.	Me haere ahau.
When will *you* come back?	A hea *koe* hoki ai (remember "koe"=1 person).
Why are *you* going?	E haere ana *koe* ki te aha?
Why should *I* go?	Ka haere *au* hei aha.
You two go.	Haere korua.
Wait for me *here/there*.	Tatari mai ki ahau i *konei/kora*.
You're too *fast/slow*.	He *tere/poturi* rawa to haere.
Hurry up!	Kia hohoro!
Are you going to *walk/go by car*?	E haere ranei koe ma te *waewae/motoka*?
Is it far from here?	Kei mamao pea?
Not far.	Kahore i matara.
Show me the way please.	Tena, whakaatu mai i te huarahi.
Who showed you the way?	Na wai i whakaatu te rori.
Where is . . . .'s house?	Kei hea te whare o . . . . ?

39

EXPRESSING EMOTIONS

I am very happy.	Ka nui te hari o toku ngakau.
I am glad/sad.	E *koa/pouri* ana ahau.
What a shame.	Katahi te mea whakama.
I was wrong.	I he taku.
I'm ashamed of you.	E whakama ana ahau ki a koe.
I don't like *him*.	E kore ahau e pirangi ki a *ia*.
I can't stand *him*.	Ka nui taku kino ki a *ia*.
You amaze me.	Ka nui taku miharo ki a koe.
I am surprised at that.	E miharo ana ahau ki tena.
Is it possible?	He pono koia?
How beautiful.	Koia ana te ataahua.
That's very pretty.	Ka nui te pai o tena.
I'm delighted with it.	E ahuareka ana ahau ki tenei.
How awful.	Ka mau te wehi.
I'm not surprised.	Ka hore ahau e miharo ana.
This/that doesn't surprise *me*.	Kahore *ahau* e miharo ki *tenei/tena*.
You don't surprise *me*.	Kahore ahau e miharo ki *tau*.
You're wrong.	E he ana *tau*.
Why are you angry/laughing?	Na te aha koe *i riri au/i pukana ai*?
My heart is broken.	Kua maru toku ngakau.
I am very sorry about this/that.	Ka nui taku pouri mo *tenei/tena*.
What a pity.	Aue, taikiri.
How annoying.	Katahi te mea whakatakirikiri.
I am tired of *you/you* are a nuisance.	Kua hoha au i a *koe*.

WEATHER

It is *hot* outside.	Ka *wera* a waho
It is very *cold*.	Ka nui te *makariri*.
It is very *hot* today.	Ka nui te *wera* o te rangi nei.
It's *warm*.	He *mahana*.
How *hot/dry/wet/cold* it is.	Ano, te nui o te *werawera/maroke/ maku/makariri*.
It will be *fine/wet* tomorrow.	Ka *paki/maku* apopo.
It is raining.	Ka ua a runga.
It is starting to rain.	Kua timata te ua.
It's fine.	He paki ano.
It's going to rain.	Me ake ka ua.
It's only a shower.	He ua noa iho.
It'll soon be over.	Meake ka mao.
It's pouring.	Ke te awha te ua.
The weather looks *bad/good*.	Ka *kino/pai* te ahua o te rangi.
What a lovely day.	Ka pai te rangi ataahua.
How is the weather outside?	Pewhea te ahua o te rangi a waho?
It is *dreadful/wonderful* weather.	He rangi *kino/pai* rawa tenei.
I'm wet through.	Kua maku rawa ahau i te ua.
My hands are frozen.	Kei te huka toku ringaringa.
The wind is *cold/warm*.	E *makariri/mahana* ana te hau.
The wind has *fallen/dropped*.	Kua *mate/huri* te hau.
If the rain stops we'll go.	Ki te mutu te *ua*, e haere ana tatou.
If it rains, I'll stay.	Ki te ua, e noho ana *au*.

ENQUIRIES

Where does he live?	Kei whea tona whare?
Where do you live?	Kei whea to whare?
Is he married?	He tangata moe wahine koia ia?
Is she married?	He wahine moe tangata koia ia?
Where is he/she?	Kei whea ia?
Where is . . . . ?	Kei whea a . . . . ?
At *work/home/the hotel* etc.	Kei te *mahi/kainga/hotera* etc.
Who showed *you* the way?	Na wai i whakaatu te rori ki a *koe*?
What's happening?	He aha te korero?
How can that be?	Ma te aha a pena ai?
What is he asking about?	He aha tena e ui mai nei?
May I ask you . . . . ?	Me ui atu pea ahau ki a koe . . . . . ?
What is *it*?	He aha *tena* (this thing near you) *tera* (that thing over there).

ENQUIRIES (*continued*)

What is that used for?	He aha *tena* mea? (Use "tena" if the object is in reasonable proximity to the person spoken to. Use "tera" if the object is a distance away.)
What do you mean?	He aha te tikanga o tau kupu?
What's the matter?	He aha tau?
Why?	Na te aha?
Who did it?	Na wai taua mahi?
Where have *you* been?	I hea *koe* e ngaro ana?
What are you doing?	He aha tau e mea nei?
Where is it?	Kei whea?
Who are you? (one person/two persons/more!	Ko wai *koe/korua/koutou*.
Is that *bad?*	He *kino/pai*, koia, tena?
Whom is this/that for?	Mo wai *tenei/tena*?
Which one is this/that?	Ko te hia *tenei/tera*?
What is the name of that *place?*	Ko hea tera?
Where is the . . . . ?	Kei whea te . . . . ?
It is not here.	Kahore i konei.
Who had that . . . . ?	I a wai tera . . . . ?
What is the time?	He aha te taima?
What is *he* doing?	Kei te aha *ia*?
What do you want?	He aha mau?
Have you a car?	Kei a koe ano he motoka?
Who lives there?	Ko wai ra te tangata e noho ana i reira?
How many (persons)?	Tokohia?
How many (things)?	Kia hia?
Are *you* there?	Kei kona ranei *koe*?
What are *you* looking for?	He aha *tau* e kimi nei?
What do *you* want?	He aha *tau* e hiahia nei?
What is *your/his* name?	Ko wai *tou/tona* ingoa?
Do *you* know him/her?	Kei te mohio *koe* ki a ia?
Who say so?	E ai ta wai?
Why are you *laughing?*	He aha tau e *kata*?
Why are *you* going to . . . . ?	He aha *koe* e hare ai ki . . . . ?
Why are *you* going?	E hare ana *koe* ki te aha?
What time will *you* get here?	A hea *koe* ka tae mai?
Where are *you* going?	Ko hea *koe*?

What is this (that—near you) (that—over there)?	He aha *tenei* (tena) (tera)?
Where is ...../Where are .....?	Kei whea ....?
What do *you* want?	He aha *to* pirangi?
Where are you going?	E haere ana koe ki hea?
I am going to Auckland.	E haere ana au ki Akarana.
Where is your friend *from*.	*No hea* to hoa?
My friend is *from Gisborne*.	*No Turanga* taku hoa.
What day is this?	Ko te aha tenei ra?
Today is *Friday*.	Ko te *Paraire* tenei ra.
What is the colour of ....?	He aha te kara o ....?
What is he/she like at ...., (any activity.)	He pehea ia ki te ....?

NEGATIVES, AFFIRMATIVES AND SHORT REPLIES

Yes.	Ae.
No.	Kahore.
Very good/o.k.	Ka nui te pai.
I don't know.	E kore ahau e mohio.
This and that.	Tenei me tena.
Never mind.	Aua atu.
I don't care.	Hei aha maku.
Be careful.	Kia tupato i a *koe* (to one person).
It is true.	He tika tonu.
I don't believe it.	Ka hore ahau i te whakapono.
I am sure of it.	Ae, ki au he pono rawa tenei.
You are right.	Ka tika *tau*.
I am wrong.	Ka he *taku*.
I agree.	Ka whakaae ahau.
Agreed.	Kua rite.
Certainly.	Koia ana.
I will do it.	Maku e mea.
Impossible.	Taikiri! e kore.
That can't be so.	E kore e pena.
That's likely.	Koia ano, tena e tika.
I don't doubt it.	Kahore e ruarua oku whakaaro.
It isn't certain.	He raruraru ano.
Nonsense!	Nukarau!
I doubt it.	Ka whakateka ahau i tenei.
I can't help it.	Te taea hoki e ahau te pewhea.
That'll do!	Kati rawa!
It doesn't matter.	Me aha, kia ahatia.

SPEAKING, HEARING AND LISTENING

You speak too fast.	He hohoro rawa to korero.
Do not speak so fast.	Kia ata haere to korero.
You speak well.	E tika ana to korero.
Do *you* speak Maori?	E korero Maori ana *koe*?
I speak it a little.	He itiiti noa iho taku mohio.
Please tell me.	Kia pai koe ki te ki mai ki ahau.
What did you say?	He aha to korero?
I cannot tell you.	E kore ahau e ahei te ki atu ki a koe.
Who told you that?	Na wai tena korero?
What do you mean?	He aha te tikanga o tau kupu?
What are you saying?	He aha tau e ki mai mei?
I do not understand you?	Kahore ahau e mohio ana ki to korero?
I don't understand Maori.	Kahore ahau e mohio.
I understand it well.	Ka nui taku mohio.
I understand Maori better than I can speak it.	Ko te mohio ki te whakarongo e mohio ana ahau, tena ko te korero e kore e tino mohio.
I don't believe what you are saying.	Ka whakateka ahau ki to korero.
Who said that?	Na wai koia ena korero?
Listen to *me/him*.	Whakarongo mai ki a *au/ia*.
I do not hear you.	Kahore ahau i te rongo i a koe.
What is your opinion?	Whakapuakina mai o whakaaro?
Tell me.	Ki mai ki a au.
Did you hear that?	I rongo ano koe ki tena?
Spell this word.	Tataungia tenei kupu.
What is the Maori word for . . . . . ?	He aha te kupu Maori mo . . . . . ?
Teach me.	Whakaakona ahau.
What do you call that/this?	He aha te ingoa o *tena/tenei* mea?
I've good/great/bad/sad news for you.	He korero *nui/pai/kino/pouri* taku.

TELLING THE TIME

In ancient times the Maoris had no clock and many will tell you with a grin that it is little change for the better to have one today. Telling the time in Maori appears complicated and many a young Maori gets over the problem when asked "He aha te taima?" (What is the time) by replying "Eight o'clock te taima!" (Eight o'clock is the time).

Here however are a few notes on the correct method of telling the time in Maori.

Vocabulary

hour	haora
minute	meneti
a.m.	o te ata (in the morning)
p.m.	o te po (in the night)
past	te pāhitanga
half past	awhepāhitanga
quarter	koata

Usage

One o'clock	Te tahi o nga haora (the first of the hours)
Ten o'clock	Te tekau o nga haora (the tenth of the hours)
It is one o'clock	Ko te tahi tenei o nga haora
.... minutes past	E te .... miniti te paahitanga o te ....
e.g. ten past seven	E te tekau miniti te paahitanga o te whitu
.... minutes to	.... miniti ki te ....
e.g. ten to seven	Tekau miniti ki te whitu
Half past four	Te awhepāhitanga o te wha
A quarter to six	Koata ki te ono
The time is *six o'clock already*	Kua *ono karaka ke* te taima
It is *nearly* 2 o'clock *already*	Kua *tata ke* te rua karaka

daytime	te awatea
night time	te po
evening	te ahiahi
afternoon	te ahiahi awatea
day and night	i te ao, i te po
midday	te poupoutanga o te ra
midnight	te waenganui po

COUNTING

To count in Maori you must use *ka* before the number:
ka rua, ka wha, ka ono = two, four, six.
To indicate a number of things use the following rules:
For one of anything—use kotahi *after* the noun
e.g. one house—he whare kotahi
For two to nine of anything—use *e* between the noun and the number
e.g. the two houses—nga whare e rua
For any number of anything above nine—use the number *after* the noun
e.g. fourteen men—he tangata kotahi tekau ma wha
For the ordinal numbers (first, second etc.) prefix the number with *te* (the)
e.g. te tahi—the first

These are the Maori numerals.
- 1 Tahi or kotahi
- 2 Rua
- 3 Toru
- 4 Wha
- 5 Rima
- 6 Ono
- 7 Whitu
- 8 Waru
- 9 Iwa
- 10 Tekau
- 11 Tekau ma tahi (i.e. ten and one).
- 12 Tekau ma rua (ten and two).
- 20 Rua tekau (i.e. two tens).
- 30 Toru tekau (three tens).
- 31 Toru tekau ma tahi (i.e. three tens and one).
- 32 Toru tekau ma rua
- 100 Kotahi rau
- 200 Rua rau
- 301 Toru rau ma tahi (i.e. three hundreds and one).
- 425 Wha rau e rua tekau ma rima (i.e. four hundreds, two tens and five).
- 1000 Kotahi mano
- 1001 Kotahi mano ma tahi
- 1021 Kotahi mano e rua tekau ma tahi etc.

Days of the Week

Monday	Mane	Friday	Paraire
Tuesday	Turei	Saturday	Hatarei
Wednesday	Wenerei	Sunday	Ratapu
Thursday	Taite		

Months of the Year

January	Hanuere	July	Hurae
February	Pepuere	August	Akuhata
March	Maehe	September	Hepetema
April	Aperira	October	Oketopa
May	Mei	November	Noema
June	Hune	December	Tihema

Seasons of the Year

Spring	Koanga	Autumn	Ngahuru
Summer	Raumati	Winter	Hotoke

Points of the Compass

North	Raro; raki	East	Rawhiti
South	Tonga	West	Hauauru; uru

47

PROVERBIAL AND POPULAR SAYINGS OF THE MAORI

The Maori has a gift of expressing himself pithily and proverbial and popular sayings are numerous. Here are just a few.
DISCRETION IS THE BETTER PART OF VALOUR
Ka karanga Taiha: "Kia apititutia! Kia whana te hingahinga nga tupapaku."
Ka karanga Maero: "E kawhakina! Tetahi momo ki te kainga."
Literally: Taiha called out: "Charge! Let's fight at close quarters so that the enemy will fall."
   Maero called out: "Let's fly away so that we may procreate to populate our village."
ONE MAN'S FOOD IS ANOTHER MAN'S POISON
He kai na te tangata, he kai titongi tongi kaki
Literally: Another man's food is food that mocks one's own appetite.
A FRIEND IN NEED IS A FRIEND INDEED
He rangatira he hoa matenga mou, kia kore koe a whakarerea.
A chief will be a friend in bad times. He will never forsake you.
A RARE VISITOR
He kotuku rerenga tahi.
The rare white heron of a single flight.
AN ONLY CHILD
Titi hua tahi.
The single egg of a mutton bird.
MANY HANDS MAKE LIGHT WORK
Ma pango, ma whero, ka oti te mahi.
Literally: By black and red the work is done. The black refers to the dirty slave and the red to the ochre with which chiefs bedaubed themselves in ancient times. At harvest time slave and chief worked alike in the cultivations to get the crop in.
GETTING ONE'S TAIL BETWEEN ONE'S LEGS
He whiore hume tenei tangata.
Literally: This man is a dog with his tail between his legs.
AS CUNNING AS A MAORI DOG
Me te kiore haumiri kakaka.
The early settlers were impressed with the cunning of the dogs in the Maori villages and coined the above English expression. The Maori however took his simile from the rat creeping along the kakaka or lattice fence which protected the kumara plantations.

A TWO FACED PERSON
He pounamu kakano rua.
A double grained piece of greenstone.

THE EARLY BIRD CATCHES THE WORM
E mua kaikai, e muri tata kino.
Early ones get the best, late ones get the spittle.

GO TO HELL!
Haere i a tuku noa i a heke noa. Mau ka oti atu, oti atu.

ONCE BITTEN, TWICE SHY
E hokihoki Kupe?
Literally: "Did Kupe ever come back? A reference to Kupe's single voyage to New Zealand.

DEAD AS A DODO
Mate a moa.
Literally: Dead as the moa. The moa was a giant native bird which was extinct by the time European settlement began in New Zealand.

KEEP YOUR TROUBLES AT HOME
E moe i to tuahine, kia kino e kino ana ki a koe ano.
Marry your cousin so that if trouble comes you will keep it to yourself.

A DEVIL ABROAD, A SAINT AT HOME
He kuku ki te kainga, he kaka ki te haere.
A pigeon at home, a parrot abroad. This refers to one who only coos when at home but who when away chatters like a parrot about everyone and everything.

MAKE HAY WHILST THE SUN SHINES
Tiketike ngahuru, hakahaka raumati.
High in autumn, low in summer, meaning that in autumn when the crops are ready food is plentiful whereas in summer's heat there is little to eat.

A BIRD IN THE HAND IS WORTH TWO IN THE BUSH
Kai mate whiwhia, maoa riro ke.
The free translation is that if you eat your food uncooked you are certain of getting it. If you wait until it is cooked someone else might get it!

WHERE THERE'S LIFE THERE'S HOPE
Iti noa ana, he pito mata.
It is only a morsel but at least it has not been cooked.

WIDE OPEN SPACES
Te taepaepatanga o te rangi.
The place where the sky reaches to the horizon.

LIKE TALKING TO THE BACK OF HIS HEAD
Kei te korero mai ki tua o te hemihemi.

DON'T COUNT YOUR CHICKENS BEFORE THEY'RE HATCHED
Whati mai. Ka eke ki te paepae poto a Hou, ki te puna whakatoto riri.
They were quick. They arrived at the very threshhold of Hou and then the fountains of war gushed over. It means that early advantage is not a guarantee of final victory.

PREVENTION IS BETTER THAN CURE
Mokonahatia te waha o te kuri nei ki te mokonaha, kei haere kei tahae.
The dog is muzzled lest it should go and steal.

PROVIDING FOR A RAINY DAY
Tukua atu ki tua, ki nga ra o te waru e.

QUALITY NOT QUANTITY
He iti ra, he iti mapihi pounamu.

Legend tells how the Ngati Porou chief Hikitai flung a spear during a battle at an opposing chief Tamahae. Tamahae taunted Hikitai because he was small and the latter replied with the above words which, loosely translated, mean: "I may be small but I am an ornament of greenstone." Greenstone of course was a most prized jade to the olden Maori.

A TROUBLE MAKER
He kuri kai tawhao.

A dog who eats scraps.

HAVING A STRING TO ONE'S BOW
Ka mate whare tahi; ka ora whare rua.

Loosely: A man with only one wife to work for him may starve. A man with two wives waxes fat. The second wife was unreliable for work on the cultivations!

TO SET ONE'S OWN HOUSE IN ORDER
Matua whakapai i tou marae, ka whakapai ai i te marae o te tangata.

Set your own place in order before cleaning up another's.

THIN SKINNED
Ngati Paoa taringa rahirahi.

Ngati Paoa of the thin ears. It implies that the tribe were sensitive to insult.

A SLIPPERY CUSTOMER
Kua kaheko te tuna i roto i aku ringaringa.

Like the eel which slips through the fingers.

FIRM AS A ROCK
Waiho i te toka tu moana.

Let it be like a rock standing in the ocean.

BE ON ONE'S GUARD
Tama tu tama ora, tama moe tama mate.

He who stands lives, he who sleeps dies.

WISHFUL THINKING
He manako te koura i kore ai.

Legend tells of the chief who took refuge in his village from an enemy. One of the enemy called: "There goes a fat meal for us." In reply the Chief called back over the palisade the above proverb: "Wishing for the crayfish will not bring it!"

BIRDS OF A FEATHER FLOCK TOGETHER
Kaore e rikarika te tama a Tumataika e rere nei.

The parrots are flocking together. (Literally, "the children of Tumataika". Tumataika was the original parrot.)

SIZE IS NOT EVERYTHING
Ahakoa he iti te matakahi, ka pakuru i a au te totara.

Although the wedge is small it will shatter the totara tree.

SOME POPULAR PLACE NAMES AND THEIR MEANINGS

There are many difficulties in taking a dictionary and literally translating a place name from Maori to English. Often the name has been derived from local myth or legend, or some allusion topical at the time, and the word can be an abbreviated reference to this incident. An example is Paeroa. "Pae" means a ridge of hills and "roa" is long. Hence it is generally thought that the place name is derived from the long range of hills which back this North Island town. In fact the derivation is quite different. "Pae" also means a transverse beam and by association, the backbone. "Paeroa" referred to the long backbone of a legendary taniwha or dragon which inhabited a stream adjacent to the site of the present town.

In other cases a place name has become corrupted over the years, thus Ruatoria should really be Rua—a—toria or "the kumara pit belonging to Toria".

Here are the generally accepted (but not always guaranteed accurate) translations of some well known place names.

AOTEAROA — The Maori name for New Zealand, said to have been given to it by the early navigator Kupe. Interpretations differ but the most commonly accepted meaning is "land of the long white cloud." Kupe is reported to have seen New Zealand as a long cloud on the horizon and his wife called "He ao (a cloud)! He ao tea (white) roa (long)."

HAURAKI — This is the great gulf East of Auckland but there are several other places of this name. "Hau" is wind and "raki" is north.

KAPITI — This is the island off Wellington's "Golden Coast". It is said to be short for Ko-te-waewae-kapiti-o-Tara-raua-ko-Rangitane or the place of the boundaries between Tara and Rangitane.

KAWERAU — The scene of today's huge paper mill derives its name from "kawe" (to carry) and "rau" (many)—thus many carriers.

MANAWATU — The fertile Manawatu district, eighty miles north of Wellington was named after a legendary incident. A long-forgotten husband Haunui was pursuing his wife for some equally forgotten reason when he came to the great river surging down through its gorge. He was so amazed that his heart stood still or in Maori "manawa-tu".

MANGAKINO — Mangakino in the heart of the North Island today is famous for its hydro electric dam. To the ancient Maori however the river was "manga" (stream) "kino" (bad).

MANAKAU — In ancient times as now this harbour was noted for its "manu" (birds) "kau" (wading).

51

MANGERE — Auckland's international jet airport terminal is inappropriately the Maori equivalent of "lazy".

MOKOIA — When Hinemoa obeyed the sounds of Tutanekai's flute and swam across the waters of Lake Rotorua to Mokoia Island she enshrined the name in Maori legend forever. However the name itself is derived from another incident in which a chief visiting the island was stabbed by a "ko" (or sharpened implement) over the eye through his "moko" or tattoo. The name is a play on the two words.

MURUPARA — The scene today of a great industry derived from the country's forests, the ancient name means "to wipe off the mud".

NGAURUHOE — There are several versions of how this mountain was named. I rather like the story of how the great sorcerer Ngatoro-i-rangi threw his grandson Hoe into the flaming crater. Thus then, as today, the belching smoke from the crater was "nga" (the) "uru" (hairs) "hoe" (of Hoe).

OHINEMUTU — When you peer at the boiling thermal pools on your visit to this part of Rotorua think of the maiden Hine-te-kakara who was murdered and thrown into one of those very pools. Her grief-stricken father called the place "o" (the place of) "hine" (the girl) "mutu" (cut short).

OTAGO — Mutilated by the early Pakeha, the name should be in Ngai Tahu dialect "Otakou" which means "o" (the place of) takou (red earth).

OTAKI — Today this fertile area is called Wellington's market garden but the ancient Maori named it "o" (the place of) "taki" (to stick in) after a warrior named Hau stuck his koikoi or spear into the ground whilst he paused to rest.

PAEKAKARIKI — "pae" (perch) kakariki (parakeets) thus—the place where parakeets perch.

PAPAKURA — Any who have visited this town and district just south of Auckland will need little imagination to realise how the Maoris derived the name of "papa" (flat) "kura" (red) or the flat land of red earth.

PONEKE — This is a transliteration of Port Nick which was the early settlers nickname for Port Nicholson, the port of Wellington.

PUTARURU — Few visitors to, or inhabitants of, this small town in the middle of the North Island would agree with the literal meaning of the Maori name. It should be spelled Puta-a-ruru and means "puta" (hole) "a" (of) "ruru" (owl).

RONGOTAI — Visitors stepping out of their aircraft at Rongotai, Wellington's airport, should listen carefully. Over the noise of arriving and departing aircraft they might hear "rongo" (sound) of the "tai" (sea).

ROTOITI — This small lake adjacent to Rotorua is aptly named "roto" (lake) "iti" (little).

ROTORUA — This was the second lake in the region to be discovered by an early Maori explorer Ihenga who naturally called it "roto" (lake) "rua" (two) or the second lake.

RUAPEHU — The highest mountain in the North Island is still active and is thus aptly called "rua" (hole) "pehu" (to explode or make a loud noise).

RUATORIA — This small town eighty miles north of Gisborne derives its name from an early incident which centred around "rua" (kumara pit) "a" (belong to) "Toria" (a man's name).

TAIERI — The district just south of Dunedin has a misspelt name. It should be "Taiari" or the tide on the eleventh night of the moon.

TARANAKI — This province famous for footballers and dairy cattle has a number of versions of how it received its Maori name. "Tara" is a mountain peak and can refer to nothing but majestic Mt Egmont. "Naki" could be 'ngaki" which means clear of vegetation.

TAUPO — The largest lake in New Zealand has also a larger name. Taupo is really short for Taupo-nui-a-Tia. This means the great cloak of Tia. Tia who discovered the lake slept beside it and likened the great flat lake to the cloak on which he slept.

TAURANGA — This popular Bay of Plenty holiday resort has an appropriate name meaning a sheltered anchorage.

TE KUITI — The name of this small King Country town through which the express trains pass late at night is actually Te Kuititanga which means the narrowing in. This probably refers to the configuration of the Mangaokewa valley at this point.

TE TAUMATA-OKIOKINGAWHAKATANGIHANGA-O-TE-KOAUAU-A-TAMATEA-POKAI-WHENUA — The longest place name in New Zealand, if not the world. The generally accepted but not strictly accurate translation is "The brow of the hill where Tamatea who sailed all around the land played his nose flute to his lady love."

TOKOROA — The name of this bustling go-ahead forestry town is simple to translate; "toko" is a pole and "roa" is long. The reason for the name however is obscure.

TONGARIRO — The third of the three mountains clustered together on the North Is. volcanic plateau gets its name from an incident involving the famous wizard Ngatoro-i-rangi who discovered the region. Sitting on top of Tongariro which was then the highest of the peaks he almost froze to death and called upon the gods in Hawaiki, far to the North, for fire. His words to them were carried by the south wind. Hence "tonga" (south wind) "riro" (carried away).

UREWERA — This wild forested area in the North Is. heartland is a derisive reference to an incident in which a chief rolled onto a fire as he slept and burnt his private parts! Thus "ure" (which Williams Dictionary delicately refers to as "membrum virile") and "wera" (burnt).

WAIKAREMOANA — This beautiful lake in the midst of the Urewera Country usually has its name translated as the sea of rippling waters.

WAIOURU — This is now the largest military camp in New Zealand. It gets its name from a small stream "wai" (water) "ouru" (of the west).

WAIOTAPU — This fascinating thermal area twenty miles south of Rotorua is aptly called "sacred waters".

WAIRAKEI — Geothermal steam gushes now from the deep bores of Wairakei. In more leisured days however the Maoris used its still pools as mirrors and christened it "wai" (water) "rakei" (adorning).

WAITANGI — This is a name bestowed on a number of places in New Zealand. The best known of these is the spot close to Russell the first capital where the Treaty of Waitangi was signed between Maori and Pakeha. The name means "wai" (water) "tangi" (weeping or noisy).

WAITEMATA — The translation of the name for Auckland's picturesque harbour is "Water like obsidian". This might have referred to its smoothness or to its dark greenish black depths.

WAITOMO — No one who has visited this fabulous area of caves will be surprised to learn that the name refers to water running underground through "tomo" or long shafts.

WHAKAREWAREWA — This most famous of New Zealand's thermal areas received its name from an incident in the past. It means in part "the uprising of the war party" and refers to a party which assembled close to the geyser and did a war dance.

WANGANUI — The correct spelling in Maori is "Whanganui" and refers to this West Coast seaport town's "whanga" (harbour) "nui" (big).

MISCELLANEOUS

Some common names and their Maori equivalents

Abraham Aperehama
Adam Atama
Allan; Alan Arena; Arana (either)
Albert Arapata
Alexander Arekahanara
Alfred Arapeti
Andrew Anaru
Ann Ani
Arthur Ata
Brownie Paraone
Carol; Carroll Kara
Carter Katene
Catherine Katarina;
Charles Taare
Cyril Hira
David Rawiri
Dorothy Tarati
Edward Eruera
Eleanor Erena
Elizabeth Irahapeti
Emily Emere
Francis Wherahiko; Paranihi
George Hori
Grey Kerei
Hanna(h) Hana
Harriett Harieta
Harold Herewini; Harawira
Henry Henare
Jack(y) (ie) Haki
James Hemi
Jane Heni
Jim(my) Himi
Joan Hoana
Jock Tioki; Tioko
John Hoani; Hone
Joseph Hohepa
Kerry Keri
Kelly Keri
King Kingi
Lana Rana

Lena Terina; Rina
Louis; Lewis Rewi
Lucy Ruihi
Mabel Mepara
Margaret Makareta
Mark Maka
Martha Mata
Mary Meri
Mary Ann Meriana
Mason Meihana
Matthew Matiu
Maud Maora
May Mei
Michael Mikaere
Morgan Mokena
Nathan Netana
Oliver; Olivier Oriwia
Paddy Paratene
Paul Paora
Peter Pita; Arapeta
Phillip Piripi
Polly Pare
Queenie Kuini
Reuben Reupena
Robert Ropata; Rapata
Ronald Renata
Samuel Hamiora
Sara Hera
Selwyn Herewini
Stephen Tipene
Susan Huhana
Sydney Hirini
Thomas Tamati
Thompson Tamiahana
Tony Toni
Walker Waaka
Walter Wara
William Wiremu
Wilson Wirihana

New Zealand Currency

New Zealand has decimal currency based on dollars (Maori—taara) and cents (Maori—heneti). Coins are one cent (1c), two cents (2c), five cents (5c) ten cents (10c), twenty cents (20c) and fifty cents (50c). There is also a one dollar ($1) coin but this coin was issued in limited quantities only for commemorative purposes. It does not circulate. The notes are one dollar ($1), two dollars ($2), five dollars ($5), ten dollars ($10), twenty dollars ($20) and fifty dollars ($50).

Metric conversion

New Zealand generally uses the metric system. For the benefit of visitors the following conversion table is given.

Inches to centimetres	multiply by 2.54
Centimetres to inches	Multiply by .39
Yards to metres	multiply by .92
Metres to yards	multiply by 1.1
Miles to kilometres	divide by 5; multiply by 8
Kilometres to miles	Divide by 8; multiply by 5
Pounds (lbs) to kilos	multiply by .45
Kilos to pounds	Multiply by 2.2
Gallons to litres	multiply by 4.54
Litres to gallons	multiply by .22

Temperature

New Zealand uses centigrade . To convert to centigrade:
Multiply by 9 then
Divide by 5 then
Add 32

Some peculiarities of local pronunciation

Englishmen and Australians have little trouble understanding New Zealanders when they meet although the New Zealand accent is as distinctive as any other. Australians tend to complain that Kiwis "whisper" and Britishers note the cockney-like twang which is becoming a disturbing feature of New Zealand speech, particularly amongst the less well educated Americans usually fail to differentiate between the speech of New Zealanders and the English probably because the pronunciation of both features the same broad "A" sound. Thus "dance" is "darnce"; "grass" is "grarss" etc.

KIWI ENGLISH

Some other aspects of the local language

Although naturally there are some regional variations, by and large New Zealanders use the same slang and colloquialisms as do other English speaking peoples. However Maori and Pakeha do use some words in a slightly different way than that to which Americans and other English speaking visitors are accustomed. A few common examples are given below. The list is by no means exhaustive.

All Black *(n)* member of New Zealand's top rugby football team.
Aussie *(n)* Australian.
Backblocks *(n)* remote area.
Bag *(n)* what Americans call "a sack".
Barrister *(n)* lawyer who appears in court.
Bach *(n)* holiday home.
Bird *(n)* girl.
Biscuit *(n)* what Americans call "cookie".
Bloke *(n)* man.
Bludger *(n)* someone who borrows but rarely returns the favour.
Bonnet *(n)* hood of a car.
Boot *(n)* trunk of a car.
Boowai or Boo-eye *(n)* the outbacks, incorrect as in "up the boowai".
Booze *(n)* hard liquor. The place where it is sold is the Boozer, Pub or Hotel.
Braces *(n)* suspenders.
Bush *(n)* the forest.
Caravan *(n)* trailer for living in.
Cattle run *(n)* ranch for beef cattle.
Cheesed off *(v)* to be fed up or upset.
Chemist shop *(n)* pharmacy.
Choice *(adj.)* excellent.
Cobber *(n)* An Australian term widely used in New Zealand to refer to one's friend or mate.
Cow Cocky *(n)* a dairy farmer.
Cocky *(n)* any type of farmer.
Crook *(n) (adj.) (v)* As a noun it has the American connotation of a criminal. As an adjective it refers to anything which is unwell, poor, shoddily manufactured. To "feel crook" is to feel sick but to be "put crook" is to "get a bum steer" or to be given misleading information.
Dag *(n)* funny fellow.
Dairy *(n)* shop selling milk, bread and groceries.
Drapery *(n)* Shop which sells cotton, material, cloth etc.
Dressing gown *(n)* bath robe.
Dummy *(n)* Pacifier for a baby, stupid person.

Flat *(n)* apartment.
Foootpath *(n)* sidewalk.
Fortnight *(n)* two weeks.
Freezing works *(n)* slaughter house.
Fridge *(n)* refrigerator.
Frock *(n)* dress.
Fruiterer *(n)* greengrocer.
Get cracking *(v)* move.
Good screw *(n)* good paycheck, good sex.
Good sport *(n)* obliging person.
Grizzle *(v)* complain.
Hardcase *(n)* humorous and slightly off beat person.
Holiday *(n)* vacation.
Homestead *(n)* ranchhouse, farm house.
Homeunit *(n)* duplex.
Housie *(n)* bingo.
Jack up *(v)* arrange.
Joker *(n)* man.
Jumper *(n)* sweater.
Kerb *(n)* curb.
Kiwi *(n)* New Zealander.
Ladder *(n)* run in stocking.
Left luggage *(n)* checked luggage.
Letter box *(n)* mail box.
Lift *(n)* elevator.
Lorry *(n)* truck.
Mate *(n)* friend as in "How are you Mate?"
Milk bar *(n)* see Dairy.
Nail varnish *(n)* nail polish.
Napkin *(n)* diapers or nappies.
Note *(n)* money bill.
Ocker *(n)* Australian.
Off the hook *(adj.)* Ready-made or out of trouble.
Old Boys/Girls *(n)* high school alumni.
Outback *(n)* rural area.
Paddock *(n)* field, meadow.
Pavement *(n)* sidewalk.
Perm *(n)* permanent hair wave.
Petrol *(n)* gasoline.
Pommie *(n)* Englishman.
Post a letter *(v)* mail a letter.
Pram *(n)* perambulator, baby carriage.
Pub *(n)* bar, hotel.
Publican *(n)* hotel manager or keeper.
Quarter past quarter after the hour.

Quarter to quarter before the hour.
Queue *(n)* line of people waiting for something.
Railway *(n)* railroad.
Reel of cotton *(n)* spool of thread.
Return ticket *(n)* round trip ticket.
Returned soldier *(n)* war veteran.
R.S.A. *(n)* Returned Services Association equivalent to the US Veterans of Foreign Wars.
Ring up *(v)* call up.
Rubber *(n)* eraser.
Rub out *(v)* erase.
Sack *(v)* *(n)* fired or a bag.
Scatty *(n)* unstable flippant person.
Scrounge *(v)* obtain something for nothing.
Serviette *(n)* table napkin.
Sheila *(n)* borrowed from Australia and meaning a woman.
She's right its O.K.
Shop *(n)* store.
Shot through *(v)* disappeared, gone away.
Shout *(v)* buy drinks.
Skite *(v)* boast.
Smoko *(n)* coffee break.
Solicitor *(n)* non-court lawyer.
Spell *(n)* rest period.
Sport *(n)* friend as in "How are you sport?"
Stalls *(n)* seats on the bottom floor of a theatre.
Stand for election *(v)* run for office.
Station *(n)* ranch.
Stiff cheese *(n)* a sarcastic term for unlucky.
Stockyard *(n)* corral.
Suspenders *(n)* garters.
Sweets *(n)* dessert or candy.
Tarmac *(n)* airport parking area for aircraft.
Teem *(v)* rain heavily.
Telephone box *(n)* telephone booth.
Too right yes indeed.
Toll call long distance call.
Town house *(n)* condominium.
Tramp *(v)* hike.
Varsity *(n)* university, college to a Kiwi is high school.
Wireless *(n)* radio.

NEW ZEALAND POCKET GUIDES

CAKE DECORATING GUIDE - Book One (S049)	Dorothy Beatty
FLORA AND FAUNA OF NEW ZEALAND (S032)	Glen Pownall
JADE TREASURES OF THE MAORI (S090)	Murdoch Riley
KIWI AND MOA - Two Unique Birds (S071)	Murdoch Riley
KIWI COOKBOOK - New Zealand Recipes (S016)	Alan Armstrong
KNOW YOUR MAORI CARVING (S069)	Glen Pownall
KNOW YOUR NEW ZEALAND BIRDS (S068)	Murdoch Riley
MAORI CUSTOMS AND CRAFTS (S009)	Alan Armstrong
MAORI LEGENDS - Retold (S017)	Alistair Campbell
MAORI LEGENDS - Japanese Edition (S099)	Alistair Campbell
MAORI SONGBOOK (S014)	Sam Freedman
MAORI VEGETABLE COOKING (S093)	Murdoch Riley
NEUSEELANDS MAORI ABC - German Edition (S098)	Murdoch Riley
NEW ZEALAND TREES AND FERNS (S073)	Murdoch Riley
NEW ZEALAND WAYS WITH FLOWERS (S075)	Eileen Dobson
NEW ZEALAND WILDLIFE - Land And Sea (S070)	Murdoch Riley
SAY IT IN MAORI - Phrase Book (S010)	Alan Armstrong
SHRUBS AND SMALL TREES (S076)	Murdoch Riley
SUCCESSFUL CAKE DECORATING - Book Two (S074)	Dorothy Beatty
WEKA WON'T LEARN - Stories For Children (S047)	Maxine Schur

NEW ZEALAND BOOKS

GAMES AND DANCES OF THE MAORI PEOPLE (B088)	Alan Armstrong
HINEMOA AND TUTANEKAI - Love Story Of Rotorua (B045)	Harold Callender
KNOW YOUR SOUTH ISLAND PLACES (B096)	Murdoch Riley
MAORI BIRD LORE - An Introduction (B100)	Murdoch Riley
MAORI GAMES - The Wisdom Of Te Wharekaihua (B039)	Colin Deed
MAORI HEALING AND HERBAL (B095)	Murdoch Riley
MAORI SAYINGS AND PROVERBS - Over 500 (B094)	Murdoch Riley
MOANA - A Novel Of Early New Zealand (B030)	Barry Mitcalfe
MUSIC OF THE MAORI - Pre-European To Modern (B034)	Terry Barrow
NEATH THE MANTLE OF RANGI - Scenic New Zealand (B036)	Brian Enting
SOLID GOLD MAORI SONGS - Words & Music 2 Songs (A053)	Sam Freedman
SURFRIDING IN NEW ZEALAND - 4th Edition (B091)	Wayne Warwick
UNIQUE NEW ZEALAND - Flora, Fauna, Maori Art (B003)	Glen Pownall
WITCH AT THE WELLINGTON LIBRARY - Children's Story (B066)	Maxine Schur

CD & CASSETTE/POCKET GUIDE COMBINATIONS

BIRDS OF NEW ZEALAND - 38 Bird Calls On Tape. With 64 page descriptive booklet on land and sea birds (VPS445CB).
Same bird calls also on CD with 12 page booklet (VPS445CD).
HAERE MAI - WELCOME! - 20 Music Tracks. With 30 page games and dances instruction booklet by Alan Armstrong (VPS475C).
POKAREKARE - 14 Music Tracks of N.Z. Maori Chorale and 60 page booklet. With words To 70 songs (VPS388CB).
25 SOLID GOLD MAORI SONGS - 25 Music Tracks On CD. With 8 page booklet of instructions in action songs, poi dance, sheet music (VPS377CD).